CURACAO TRAVEL GUIDE 2024

Curacao Unveiled With Map & Images:Discover The Best Beaches,Caves,Things To Do With Perfect Itinerary,Best Hotels,Food,History & Cultural Heritage.

Christie J. Wells

Table of Contents

A Journey into the Heart of Colorful Contrasts.

As I arrived at the sun-kissed dunes of Curaçao, a wave of adrenaline and awe flowed over me. The island greeted me with open arms, its brilliant energy echoing the kaleidoscope of colors that covered its streets, houses, and even the local smiles. I couldn't help but feel an immediate connection to this land of contrasts, where history intertwines with modernity, and where the past and present dance in harmony.

As I strolled through the streets of Willemstad, the capital city, I found myself surrounded by a wonderful combination of architectural styles. The magnificent Dutch colonial façade stood proudly, revealing their past, but the vivid tones of blue, pink, and yellow changed them into living, breathing artworks.

The majestic Queen Emma Bridge, widely known as the "Swinging Old Lady," linked the two sides of the city, slowly rotating to allow boats to pass through. It was a spectacle that perfectly underlined the island's capacity to meld legacy and modernity.

Amidst the bustling bustle of the floating market, where boats packed with fresh vegetables and spices jostled for attention, I engaged in a severe quarrel with a local seller. His memories gave a vivid picture of Curaçao's evolution, as he recalled stories of his forefathers and their tenacity in the face of sorrow. The convergence of cultures - African, European, and Caribbean - had woven a beautiful tapestry of rituals, customs, and cuisines that filled the air with a sense of oneness.

Venturing beyond the city, I encountered the hidden beauties that Curaçao holds dear. The crystal-clear waters of Grote Knip Beach surrounded me, tempting me to enjoy the peace of nature's workmanship. As I swam in the warm embrace of the Caribbean Sea, I received an overwhelming feeling of thanks for the immaculate beauty that surrounded me.

The island's heart beats to the rhythm of its spectacular festivals, and I was fortunate enough to observe the intensity of Carnival. Colorful parades, enticing music, and spectacular costumes filled the streets, and I couldn't help but immerse myself in the pulse of the celebration. Dancing with locals, I appreciated the easygoing vibe that Curaçao freely bestows upon its tourists.

Yet, beyond the festivities and the breathtaking scenery, it was the warmth of the people that had an indelible imprint on my heart. Every connection looked like a true sharing of stories and laughter, reminding me that in this Technicolor paradise, friendships are made with honesty.

As you travel on your own voyage across Curaçao, may you unearth the magic that waits beneath its opposites? Let the past speak its secrets as the present envelops you in its joyous embrace. Welcome to a place where history and culture blend, where hidden treasures await your investigation, and where the island's pulse resonates with your own.

What to Expect from This Guide

What to Expect from This Guide: Your Key to Unlocking the Wonders of Curaçao.

Welcome to a voyage of discovery as we dive into the depths of Curaçao, an island paradise that beckons with its rich history, vibrant culture, magnificent scenery, and exciting activities. This guide is your trustworthy companion, prepared to take you on a lovely trip through the heart and soul of this Caribbean gem.

Comprehensive Insights and Insider Knowledge:

Prepare to embark on an intensive tour, as this book goes beyond the surface to offer you profound insights into every area of Curaçao. From its colonial past to its modern-day vitality, you'll study the layers that contribute to its unique identity. Gain access to insider knowledge, interlaced with personal experiences and local opinions, ensuring you're equipped with a thorough grasp of the island's character.

A Tapestry of History and Culture:
Unravel the threads of history that have fashioned Curaçao into the intriguing tapestry it is today. Explore the island's rich history, following the footsteps of explorers and those who created their mark. Immerse yourself in its rich culture, from tasty regional foods to rhythmic dances that depict the spirit of the celebration. Every page will unveil a fresh tale, allowing you to connect with Curaçao's past and present in meaningful ways.

Guided Exploration of Must-See Attractions:
Embark on a virtual tour of Curaçao's must-see monuments, precisely planned to guarantee you experience the greatest the island has to offer. Wander through the vivid alleyways of Willemstad, where architectural jewels endure as living testaments to a bygone history. Bask in the magnificence of sun-drenched beaches and tranquil coves, where blue waters meet perfect dunes. Marvel at historic places and engage with people, discovering the essence of this unique city.

Unveiling Hidden Gems & Local Treasures:
Venture off the conventional route with confidence, as this book unveils Curaçao's hidden treasures waiting to be found. Experience the excitement of adventure as you explore serene landscapes, visit attractive settlements, and find hidden havens. Whether you're seeking serene contemplation or wild escapades, these lesser-known beauties develop a real and deep contact with the island.

Insider's Tips for a Seamless Experience:
Navigate Curaçao like a seasoned tourist with expert suggestions and assistance that cater to your every need. From practical travel information to cultural etiquette, safety requirements, and sustainable travel practices, you'll be well-prepared for a wonderful and pleasurable holiday. Delve into crucial words in Papiamento, the

local language, to develop true connections and immerse yourself in the island's warm embrace.

Tailored Itineraries and Travel Planning:
Craft your ideal schedule with the assistance of well-chosen selections that appeal to varied interests and tastes. Whether you're a history buff, a nature enthusiast, an adventure seeker, or a cultural expert, you'll uncover specific ideas to construct a personalized and enjoyable trip. Learn about the optimal times to visit, activities to look out for, and crucial items to carry, ensuring a stress-free and happy holiday.

Embark on Your Curaçao Adventure:
As you embark on this literary adventure throughout Curaçao, allow your senses to be tantalized, your curiosity stimulated, and your wanderlust gratified. This book is your key to unlocking the joys that await, presenting you with a method to explore, discover, and appreciate the moments that distinguish a wonderful journey. So, open the page and fall into a world of color, culture, and unique experiences. Your Curaçao journey begins now.

Practical Travel Information

Navigating Your Way through Curaçao with Ease.

Preparing for a visit to Curaçao entails more than just packing your luggage; it's about providing yourself with the practical knowledge that will make your travel smooth and joyful. In this comprehensive chapter, we'll look at the crucial travel information you need to ensure a flawless vacation in this lovely island paradise.

Entry and Visa Requirements:
Before setting foot on Curaçao, confirm you have the proper papers. validate the visa requirements based on your nationality and ensure your passport is valid for the duration of your trip.

Currency & Money Matters:
Curaçao's currency is the Netherlands Antillean guilder (ANG), yet the U.S. dollar is commonly recognized. Familiarize yourself with currency conversion rates, and be aware of bringing a mix of cash and cards for diverse costs.

Language and Communication:
While Dutch is the official language, many locals also speak English and Papiamento. Having a few basic phrases in Papiamento may broaden your relations and demonstrate your love for the local culture.

Health and Safety:
Prioritize your well-being by familiarizing yourself with health and safety information. bring any important prescriptions, pack a first aid kit, and be hydrated in the tropical heat. It's necessary to have travel insurance that covers medical concerns.

Vaccinations and Health Precautions:
Check with your healthcare practitioner for necessary immunizations before traveling to Curaçao. Protect yourself against mosquito-borne diseases by using insect repellent and wearing adequate clothing.

Local Customs & Etiquette:
Respect local customs and traditions via understanding the cultural norms. Greet neighbors with a cordial "bon bini" (welcome), and ask for permission before capturing photographs of persons or their property.

Transportation:
Navigate the island with comfort by researching the transportation possibilities. Renting a car allows flexibility, although taxis and buses are also available. Remember that traffic moves on the right side of the road.

Accommodation Options:
Choose from a range of accommodations, including luxury resorts, boutique hotels, guesthouses, and vacation rentals. Research and secure your dream hotel in advance to have the greatest alternatives.

Electricity and Plug Types:
Curaçao utilizes Type A and Type B electrical outlets with a voltage of 127V/50Hz. Depending on your home country, you may need a plug adapter or voltage converter.

Time Zone:
Curaçao follows Atlantic Standard Time (AST), which is UTC-4. Be careful of the time difference and alter your plans accordingly.

Internet and Communication:
Stay connected by verifying the availability of Wi-Fi at your hotel and public areas. Consider purchasing a local SIM card or an overseas data subscription for your mobile smartphone.

Shopping and Souvenirs:
Explore local markets and companies to locate rare souvenirs, crafts, and goods. Be careful of duty-free privileges when returning to your home country.

Tipping and Service Charges:
Tipping is customary in Curaçao. Check whether a service charge is included on your account, and consider leaving an extra tip for exemplary treatment.

Emergency Contacts:
Save crucial contact numbers, including local emergency services, your embassy or consulate, and your accommodation's front desk.

Armed with this crucial travel information, you're positioned to start on your Curaçao adventure prepared. As you traverse the island's diverse landscapes and engage with its charming people, your voyage will be heightened by the confidence that comes from knowing you can make the most of every encounter. Embrace the beauty, culture, and experiences that await you, and make your Curaçao cruise a monument to the power of well-prepared travel.

Tracing the Footsteps of Curaçao's History.

Curaçao's interesting tale is artfully linked with threads of colonial history that have left a lasting imprint on the island's character. Embarking on a trip through its colonial past is like turning the pages of a difficult and puzzling book, where different cultures, opposing forces, and lingering legacies have combined to make the rich tapestry that is modern-day Curaçao.

A Confluence of Empires:
The annals of Curaçao's colonial history began in the early 16th century when Spanish explorers first set their eyes on its coasts. The island's strategic location made it a sought-after prize, leading to a tug-of-war between European powers. It was the Dutch, meanwhile, who finally constructed a firm basis. In 1634, they captured Curaçao from the Spanish, and the island became an important hub for trade and commerce in the Caribbean.

The Dutch Influence:
Under Dutch sovereignty, Curaçao emerged as a significant commercial port. The natural harbor of Willemstad aided the trafficking of cargoes, and the Dutch West India Company maintained a large presence on the island. This impact is still obvious today,

particularly in the colonial architecture that graces Willemstad's streets. The characteristic pastel-colored buildings, reminiscent of Dutch urban architecture, survive as a tribute to the island's continuous connections with its colonial origins.

A Mosaic of Cultures:
Curaçao's history is not simply inspired by Dutch influence; it's a vibrant mosaic of cultures and peoples. The Dutch brought enslaved Africans to the island to work on plantations, and their presence has dramatically influenced Curaçao's cultural fabric. This blend of African, European, and Indigenous components has given rise to a unique identity that is portrayed in language, cuisine, music, and traditions.

Language and Identity:
One of the most famous vestiges of Curaçao's colonial history is the formation of Papiamento, a Creole language that arose as a medium of communication among enslaved Africans and European colonists. Over time, Papiamento emerged as a symbol of cultural identity, a monument to the resilience of a people who constructed a language from diverse linguistic roots.

Heritage & Preservation:
Exploring Curaçao's colonial past requires journeying back in time via its historic sites. Willemstad's UNESCO-listed historic neighborhoods, Punda and Otrobanda, are living testaments to the island's heritage. Forts, such as Fort Amsterdam and Fort Nassau, remain

like tranquil sentinels, providing perspectives into a bygone period when these defenses defended the island from sea invasions.

Embracing the Past, Shaping the Future:
Curaçao's colonial past is not restricted to the pages of history; it lives on via the island's traditions, celebrations, and way of life. The awareness of this past has led to steps to safeguard and promote Curaçao's cultural heritage. Museums, such as the Curaçao Maritime Museum and the Museum Kura Hulanda, provide unique insights into the island's past, providing a bridge between generations and fostering a lovely sense of pride in Curaçao's special character.

Tracing Curaçao's colonial past is a tour of inquiry, learning, and pleasure. It's an opportunity to connect with the island's past, to sense the persistence of its people, and to appreciate the unique combination of cultures that defines Curaçao today. As you explore its historic streets, immerse yourself in its history, and connect with its people, you'll begin to appreciate the rich tapestry of influences that have fashioned this spectacular Caribbean destination.

Road to Independence

Curaçao's Quest for Autonomy and Self-Determination.

Curaçao's march to freedom is a testimony to the island's resilience, endurance, and developing identity. From its colonial past to its modern-day objectives, the route to independence has been defined by battles, victories, and a deep-seated longing for self-determination.

Colonial Legacy and Struggles:
Curaçao's history as a trade outpost under Dutch sovereignty set the basis for its final struggle for independence. While the island prospered as a center of commerce, the scars of slavery and imperial cruelty remained deeply ingrained. The challenges and injustices suffered by the local community throughout history created the foundations of a longing for autonomy and a role in shaping their destiny.

Evolving Identity and Cultural Pride:
As Curaçao's cultural identity started to grow, a sense of pride and togetherness evolved among its diversified people. Papiamento, the Creole language that embodies endurance, became a fantastic vehicle for protecting and celebrating the island's heritage. Local customs, festivals, and rituals further underlined the particular character that would play a major role in the war for independence.

Political Awakening and Demands for Change:
The second half of the 20th century witnessed an age of significant political awakening in Curaçao. The desire for more autonomy and a voice in decision-making gained

traction. The people of Curaçao desired a future where they could choose their direction, free from outside constraints.

Path to Self-Governance:
In 1954, Curaçao, along with the other islands of the Netherlands Antilles, accomplished a significant milestone with the installation of a new constitutional framework that granted them a degree of self-governance within the Kingdom of the Netherlands. This was a step towards autonomy when Curaçao won the power to control several areas of its internal affairs.

Toward a New Political Status:
As the years passed, the need for even greater autonomy and self-determination continued to increase. In 2005, Curaçao, along with Sint Maarten, became independent entities within the Kingdom of the Netherlands, each having its government and constitution. This measure was a big move towards a more independent attitude, offering Curaçao greater autonomy over its economic, social, and political challenges.

The Challenges of Independence:
While the route to independence has been one of wealth and triumph, it has also been defined by setbacks. Economic stability, social progress, and international recognition are among the concerns that Curaçao must handle as it continues to create its future as an independent country.

A Bright Future Ahead:

As Curaçao travels the route to independence, its narrative serves as an example to other nations eager to construct their destiny. The island's story displays the power of unity, cultural pride, and unwavering tenacity. While problems remain ahead, the spirit of Curaçao's people is unshakable, and the aim of a future marked by autonomy and self-governance lights brightly on the horizon.

Curaçao's road to freedom is a narrative of transformation, a story of a people who have risen beyond past limits to forge their way. As Curaçao continues to construct its own story, the island's path serves as a reminder that the desire for autonomy, self-determination, and a better future is a common ambition that transcends borders and generations.

Cultural Heritage and Identity

Unveiling the Soul of Curaçao.

Curaçao's cultural heritage is a treasure trove that brings together centuries of history, diversity, and inventiveness. It's a celebration of the island's past, a reflection of its present, and a promise for its future. From its charming rituals to its lively festivals, Curaçao's cultural identity is a patchwork of influences that have come together to produce a rich and appealing tapestry.

The Fusion of Cultures:

At the basis of Curaçao's cultural identity is its unique blend of cultures. The island's colonial history drew together African, European, and Indigenous components, resulting in a harmonic combination that is both distinctive and harmonious. This combination is obvious in every element of Curaçao's culture, from its languages and music to its cuisine and architecture.

Papiamento: The Language of Unity:
One of the most noteworthy manifestations of Curaçao's cultural diversity is the Creole language, Papiamento. Born from the necessity of communication among various tribes, Papiamento is a linguistic beauty that represents the tenacity and oneness of the people. Its rhythmic cadence is a symbol of the island's identity, transcending borders and serving as a source of pride for Curaçaoans.

Traditional Music and Dance:
Music is the heartbeat of Curaçao, a worldwide language that speaks to the soul. Traditional music, such as tumba and waltz, reverberates through the streets during festivals and celebrations, luring both locals and visitors to dance to its captivating rhythms. Tambú, a passionate dance based on African traditions, conveys themes of resistance and empowerment through movement and song.

Culinary Delights: A Taste of Tradition:
Curaçao's culinary culture is a testimony to its rich past. The island's cuisine is a wonderful blend of tastes,

containing dishes that reflect African, European, and Indigenous cultures. Indulge in rich stews, great seafood, and vibrant tropical fruits that are not only a feast for the senses but also a tour through history.

Festivals & Celebrations: A Spirited Showcase:
Curaçao's vivid festivals and celebrations are a dynamic expression of its cultural past. Carnival, a spectacular show of color, music, and dance, is a monument to the island's enthusiasm for life and innovation. The Seú parade, held during Carnival, pays tribute to the challenges of the past while celebrating the victory of the human spirit.

Art and Craftsmanship: Expression and Identity:
Local artists and artisans contribute to Curaçao's cultural past via their creative expressions. Intricate beading, pottery, and other handicrafts express the island's cultural narratives, perpetuating traditions that have been passed down through years. The art scene in Curaçao is a vibrant canvas where current artists merge their work with the island's character.

Cultural Preservation and Future Aspirations:
As Curaçao navigates the currents of modernity, cultural preservation is a key task. Efforts to retain old practices, architectural marvels, and indigenous knowledge are a tribute to the island's devotion to honoring its heritage. These activities are related to goals for a future that honors tradition while embracing innovation.

Curaçao's cultural legacy and identity are the bedrock of the island, a rich mosaic that embodies the spirit of solidarity, variation, and tenacity. As you learn Curaçao's traditions, enjoy its cuisines, and immerse yourself in its festivals, you'll uncover the essence of a people who have fashioned a living and dynamic identity through the fabric of time. In every note of music, in every brush of painting, and every step of dance, you'll find the heart of Curaçao's cultural past pounding with a pulse that is as timeless as it is beautiful.

Culinary Delights and Local Cuisine

Savoring the Flavors of Curaçao.

Keshi Yena is a traditional dish from Curacao that exhibits the island's rich culinary history. Its name, which means "stuffed cheese" in Papiamento, properly characterizes the production of this tasty pleasure. The meal began during the colonial period when the Dutch immigrants relished the creamy insides of cheese wheels, leaving the skin. The inhabitants, not wanting to waste food, cleverly utilized the hollowed-out cheese wheel as a vessel to prepare a substantial and savory stew.

The recipe entails filling the hollowed-out cheese with a combination of meats, often chicken or goat, and a potpourri of fragrant spices. The filling may comprise a mix of onions, bell peppers, tomatoes, olives, capers, raisins, and other spices, producing a powerful and well-seasoned composition. The packed cheese is then baked until it develops a golden-brown crust, resulting in a unique combination of melting cheese and savory, fragrant delight.

Keshi Yena is not only a wonderful expression of Curacao's blend of culinary influences but also a sign of ingenuity and inventiveness in the kitchen. It serves as a tribute to the island's capacity to convert modest materials into a meal that captivates the taste senses with its rich and delicious tastes. This meal is commonly offered at important events and family gatherings, making it a valued component of Curacaoan cuisine.

Funchi is a typical dish in Curaçaoan cuisine, and it's a basic element of many meals on the island. This basic but flexible side dish is composed of cornmeal, water, and salt. The preparation entails heating water, gradually adding cornmeal while stirring continually to prevent lumps, and then letting the liquid thicken. The outcome is a thick, somewhat sticky, and smooth consistency.

Once cooked, fungi may be shaped into different forms, typically acting as a delicious addition to stews, fish, or meat meals. Its mild taste makes it an ideal accompaniment to the rich and delicious main dishes prevalent in Curaçaoan cuisine.

Whether served in slices or as a soft mound on the plate, fungi add a lovely texture and a touch of comfort to the bright palette of tastes that characterize the culinary experience in Curaçao.

Stoba is a classic Caribbean dish that is popular in Curacao. It often involves slow-cooked meat, frequently beef or goat, mixed with a thick and savory sauce. The meal is distinguished by a savory combination of herbs and spices, including cumin, coriander, and garlic, giving it a unique flavor. Stoba is commonly eaten with sides like rice, beans, or fungi, a cornmeal-based side dish. The lengthy cooking method lets the flavors mingle, resulting in a rich and comforting meal that symbolizes the culinary legacy of Curacao.

Pastechi is a popular and savory snack in Curaçao, consisting of a deep-fried pastry filled with different delectable contents. The pastry is often produced using a dough that contains flour, butter, and water, giving a crispy and golden surface. The contents may vary and may include spicy meats like chicken, beef, or goat, along with components like cheese, ham, or fish. Pastechi is consumed throughout the day and is a tasty expression of Curaçao's many culinary traditions.

Ayaka is a traditional meal in Curaçao, frequently savored during festive events such as Christmas. It comprises a savory combination of seasoned meat, often chicken or pig, coupled with raisins, olives, capers, and occasionally vegetables. This combination is wrapped in a banana leaf, fastened tightly, and then boiled or steamed. The banana leaf lends a distinct scent and taste to the meal. Ayaka is treasured for its delicious flavor and the cultural importance it carries in Curaçaoan cuisine.

Kabritu, commonly known as Curry Goat, is a traditional meal in Curaçao and several Caribbean nations. It comprises goat meat that's seasoned and slow-cooked to perfection in a fragrant curry sauce. The recipe often contains a variety of fragrant spices such as curry powder, thyme, garlic, and scallions. The goat flesh is frequently marinated beforehand to enable the taste to permeate deeply.

Once marinated, the meat is slow-cooked until soft, enabling it to absorb the rich curry aromas. The outcome is a savory and fragrant meal with a distinct flavor. Kabritu is commonly served with a side of rice and beans, adding to the substantial and comforting aspect of the dish.

This recipe not only demonstrates the impact of Caribbean culinary traditions but also illustrates the ingenuity of utilizing locally accessible products, since goat meat is a prevalent protein source in the area. Kabritu is a tasty and culturally important meal that highlights the variety of Caribbean cuisine.

Arena di Pampuna, commonly known as Pumpkin Pancake, is a classic dish from Curaçao that showcases the island's rich culinary history. This delectable pancake is cooked using pumpkin as a key ingredient, giving it a particular taste and a vivid orange tint. The use of locally produced pumpkins gives a touch of freshness and a distinctive flavor to this famous meal.

The preparation requires blending or mashing pumpkin into a smooth puree, which is then blended with components like flour, sugar, cinnamon, and occasionally nutmeg. The resultant batter is fried on a griddle or in a skillet until golden brown and cooked through. The inclusion of toasty spices lends to the pancake's fragrant and warming appeal.

Arena di Pampuna is commonly appreciated as a breakfast or snack food. It may be eaten on its own, sprinkled with powdered sugar, or accompanied with a dollop of whipped cream. Some varieties may use raisins or nuts for extra texture and taste.

This meal not only shows the local products of Curaçao but also illustrates the island's cultural blend, since it takes inspiration from African, European, and indigenous culinary traditions. It's a great example of how Curaçao's food reflects the variety and history of the island.

Bolo Pretu, or "Black Cake" in Papiamento, is a classic fruit dessert that occupies a unique position in Curacao's culinary legacy. Prepared mainly for celebratory events like weddings and holidays, it's distinguished by its rich, dark hue and thick texture. The cake is constructed with a blend of dried fruits, such as raisins and currants, steeped in local liquor or rum for a lengthy time. Molasses or brown sugar adds to its rich color, and different spices give a culinary depth. Bolo Pretu is commonly savored as a celebration dessert, conveying both cultural meaning and a delicious flavor.

Yuana, also known as Iguana Stew, is a traditional meal in Curaçao cooked from the flesh of the green iguana.

The iguana is frequently marinated and then cooked with a delicious combination of herbs and spices. The final meal is recognized for its rich and slightly gamey flavor. Yuana has cultural importance on the island, and although it may not be to everyone's taste owing to the unusual flavor, it's regarded as a delicacy by those who prefer local, traditional food in Curaçao.

Sòpi Mondongo is a typical Caribbean soup, popularly consumed in Curacao. The meal contains mondongo, which is tripe (the lining of a cow's stomach) and is commonly made with a variety of vegetables such as bell peppers, celery, carrots, and potatoes. The soup is spiced with herbs and spices, producing a thick and flavorful broth. It's a hearty and culturally important meal, highlighting the island's culinary variety.

Culinary Delights: Exploring Curaçao's Gastronomic Scene.

When it comes to relishing in the culinary delights of Curaçao, you're in for an incredible gastronomic experience that symbolizes the island's rich cultural tapestry. As I strolled into the heart of Curaçao's dining scene, I discovered a profusion of restaurants that offered not only exceptional food but also a profound relationship to the island's history and culture.

Mosa is a prominent restaurant situated in Willemstad, Curacao. Known for its exquisite decor and waterfront location, Mosa provides a broad cuisine that mixes cosmopolitan tastes with a touch of Caribbean influence. The restaurant is located in the fashionable Pietermaai District, enabling guests to enjoy their meals with breathtaking views of the Caribbean Sea. Mosa is famous for its fresh seafood meals, excellent service, and relaxing setting that embodies the spirit of Curacao's culinary scene.

Fort Nassau is a historic restaurant set on a hill overlooking Willemstad, the capital of Curaçao. Located on the remains of an 18th-century fort, the restaurant provides not only a gourmet experience but also panoramic views over the island and its dynamic city. Fort Nassau is noted for its eclectic cuisine, which mixes foreign and local dishes, producing a unique dining experience. The site delivers a wonderful combination of history, architecture, and natural beauty, making it a popular option for both residents and tourists seeking a memorable gastronomic and visual experience.

The Wine Cellar is a notable restaurant in Willemstad, Curacao. Located in the historic Pietermaai District, it provides a unique dining experience in a beautifully renovated 18th-century home. The restaurant is famous for its large variety of wines, both foreign and local, and its cozy environment. The cuisine boasts a combination of Mediterranean and Caribbean tastes, and diners may enjoy their meals outside a picturesque courtyard setting or inside the stylishly designed interior. The Wine Cellar is a popular option for people wanting a gourmet cuisine experience with a hint of historic charm.

Kome is a prominent restaurant situated in Willemstad, the capital of Curaçao. It is noted for its unique and modern approach to Caribbean and international food. The restaurant focuses on utilizing fresh, local ingredients to make excellent meals. Kome's cuisine generally incorporates a blend of culinary styles, delivering a unique eating experience. The location in Willemstad adds to the attractiveness, enabling guests to experience not just superb cuisine but also the colorful ambiance of the island's capital.

As of my recent knowledge update in September 2021, I don't have particular information regarding a restaurant called "Nultwintig" in Curacao. It's conceivable that this restaurant may be a new business or one that I don't know information about.

For accurate and up-to-date information, including the location and specifics about Nultwintig in Curacao, I suggest checking internet review platforms, the restaurant's website, or contacting local tourist sources for the latest information.

Zest Mediterranean is a renowned restaurant in Willemstad, Curacao. It is noted for its Mediterranean-inspired food, providing a broad menu with dishes influenced by the cuisines of nations such as Greece, Italy, and Spain. The restaurant is famous for its fresh ingredients, unique cooking, and a dynamic dining scene. Zest Mediterranean is widely lauded for its seafood choices, grilled meats, and a range of vegetarian alternatives. The location offers a sophisticated and pleasant environment, making it a preferred site for residents and tourists wishing to enjoy a unique Mediterranean eating experience in the heart of Willemstad.

Restaurant Gouverneur de Rouville is an elite eating restaurant located in the center of Willemstad, the capital city of Curaçao. Located in a magnificent colonial structure in the historic town of Pietermaai, the restaurant provides an exquisite setting with a combination of European and Caribbean elements. Known for its culinary quality, Gouverneur de Rouville presents a diversified cuisine comprising a mix of foreign and local foods, presented with a unique touch. The site offers a unique eating experience, enabling clients to enjoy their meals in a sophisticated environment while immersing themselves in the historic atmosphere of the gorgeous Pietermaai region.

Fishalicious is a prominent seafood restaurant situated in Willemstad, Curacao. Known for its concentration on fresh, high-quality seafood, the restaurant provides a broad menu offering a range of fish and shellfish dishes. With a reputation for inventive and tasty preparations, Fishalicious presents a dining experience that accentuates the riches of the sea. The restaurant is located in the center of Willemstad, enabling guests to experience both the culinary pleasures and the attractive ambiance of the ancient capital of Curacao.

Jaanchie's Restaurant is a well-known institution in Westpunt, Curaçao. Famous for its laid-back environment and local charm, Jaanchie's is recognized for providing traditional Caribbean meals, including fresh fish. One of its specialties is iguana soup, bringing a distinctive twist to the cuisine. The restaurant is also noted for its relaxed environment and the friendly warmth of the personnel. The location in Westpunt provides a more peaceful and picturesque setting, making it a favorite site for both residents and tourists seeking a genuine experience of Curaçao.

Equus is a popular restaurant in Curaçao, recognized for its upmarket dining experience and a specialty in grilled meats, notably steaks. The restaurant is famous for its classy decor, excellent service, and a broad cuisine that appeals to meat lovers. Equus is situated in the area of Willemstad, the capital of Curaçao, providing a refined environment for guests seeking a high-quality eating experience.

Equus is located in a fantastic position, only a short drive from Willemstad's busy city center. The restaurant typically impresses guests with its modern design, providing a welcoming environment for both residents and tourists. As a steakhouse, Equus takes pleasure in obtaining exceptional cuts of meat and creating a cuisine that shows a dedication to culinary excellence. The combination of its central location, elegant atmosphere, and concentration on top-notch food makes Equus a distinctive dining destination in Curaçao.

Rhythms of Heritage: Traditional Music and Dance of Curaçao.

As I immersed myself in the colorful culture of Curaçao, the captivating rhythms of traditional music and the rhythmic movements of dancing became the soundtrack of my voyage. The island's rich history and diverse influences were beautifully woven into the fabric of its traditional music and dance, generating a tapestry of melodies and motions that spoke volumes about its people and their lasting spirit.

Tambú: A Celebration of Resilience.
Tambú, the lifeblood of Curaçao's traditional music, pulled me in with its pounding beats and exquisite melodies. I had the honor of attending a Tambú performance in the center of Willemstad, where expert players played drums, shakers, and rasps with incredible accuracy. The music portrayed stories of resistance, persistence, and victory over suffering, mirroring the island's history of defeating challenges. As I joined locals in screaming and dancing to the beat, I felt a great connection to Curaçao's past and a tremendous admiration for the fortitude of its people.

Danza: The Elegance of Island Life.
Danza, a traditional dance technique, moved me to a degree of beauty and elegance. The dancers' routines were a visual reflection of Curaçao's distinctive heritage, with European and African components skillfully blended. I had the privilege of seeing a Danza performance at a local festival when dancers dressed in gorgeous costumes hovered over the stage. Their excellent footwork and expressive moves conveyed stories of love, joy, and the common experiences of the island's people. It was a reminder that dancing is not merely a source of pleasure but an essential technique for conserving and transmitting cultural narratives.

Serenade and Waltz: Echoes of the Past.
While Tambú and Danza are firmly based in Curaçao's history, I learned that the island's cultural identity is a great blend of cultures. Attending a serenade performance, where musicians serenaded couples with wonderful melodies, restored me to a bygone age of wooing and gallantry. The waltz, a European import, was skillfully done by dancers who readily matched its exact moves with the island's vibrant splendor. These events displayed the immaculate combination of numerous ethnic traits that make Curaçao's music and dance so unique.

Local Encounters: Embracing the Rhythms.
One evening, I had the privilege of joining a group of locals for an impromptu dance session by the coast. As the sun sank and the sky turned into a painting of colors,

we formed a circle and danced to the rhythm of Tambú. The laughter, the connecting, and the shared joy transcended linguistic borders, reminding me of the universal language that is music and dancing. It was a time of utter delight, when ethnic borders evaporated, and we celebrated life together through dancing and singing.

Preserving Tradition, Embracing Evolution.
Curaçao's traditional music and dance serve as a bridge between generations, retaining historical knowledge while adapting to the contemporary world. Festivals and cultural events continue to exhibit these colorful creative forms, allowing both locals and visitors to sense the essence of the island. The wonderful blend of history and innovation symbolizes Curaçao's desire to honor its past while embracing its future.

A Symphony of Culture.
My excursion to Curaçao's traditional music and dance was a symphony of emotions, a testimony to the power of artistic expression in establishing cultural identity. The island's rhythms and movements rang with stories of triumph, love, and unity, offering a powerful connection between the past and the present. As I left Curaçao, the echoes of Tambú, the beauty of Danza, and the enchantment of serenades remained to dance in my heart, a reminder that the essence of a region is sometimes best experienced via its music and dance.

A Creative Expression of Curaçao's Soul.

As I strolled farther into the heart of Curaçao's cultural environment, I noticed that the island's creative force is as lively and diverse as its residents. From beautiful beading to colorful paintings that seem to move with life, Curaçao's arts and crafts provide a fascinating portrait of its past, present, and future.

Beadwork: A Labor of Love and Tradition.
I had the honor of observing the making of beautiful beading by a local artist. As I watched the fast fingers weave bright beads into intricate shapes, I was astounded by the passion and talent required to bring these wonders to life. Each sculpture conveyed a narrative, a testament to the creative genius and the rich heritage that has been passed down through millennia. The beading, whether decorating clothes or ornamental objects, appeared like a direct link to Curaçao's history and a lively statement of its cultural identity.

Visual Arts: A Canvas of Color and Emotion.
Walking around Curaçao's galleries and art venues, I was amazed by the kaleidoscope of colors that covered the artworks. The island's natural beauty, historical attractions, and everyday life were all wonderfully represented, each stroke of the brush capturing the spirit of Curaçao's character. One particular artwork jumped out to me — a portrayal of Willemstad's usual

pastel-colored houses placed against the backdrop of a blazing sunset. The artwork seeks to emit warmth and nostalgia, a real appreciation of the island's architectural magnificence and the sensations it elicits.

Pottery and Handicrafts: Preserving Tradition.
In a tiny workshop, I observed a skilled artist shaping clay into gorgeous ceramics. The goods exhibited magnificent designs inspired by Curaçao's flora, wildlife, and cultural motifs. The artist underlined that pottery was not merely a creative activity but also a method of perpetuating Curaçao's cultural themes and practices. Holding a piece of Curaçaoan pottery, I felt a link to the island's past, a real kinship to the hands that had fashioned its history.

Sculptures and Installations: A Sense of Wonder.
Curaçao's public areas are decorated with sculptures and installations that promote contemplation and provoke curiosity. One sculpture, in particular, drew my attention - a breathtaking depiction of oneness and variation, with individuals linked in a dance of peace. As I inspected the artwork, I couldn't help but focus on the island's path of cultural fusion and the message of oneness it portrays.

Cultural Workshops: Engaging in Creativity.
Participating in a local arts and crafts class enabled me to immerse myself in the creative process. Guided by expert instructors, I tried my hand at beading and pottery, getting a deeper respect for the intricacy and

talent required to accomplish these crafts. Engaging in these hands-on activities boosted my understanding of Curaçao's cultural legacy and left me with a sense of success and connection.

Curaçao's arts and crafts are more than simply artistic expressions; they are windows into the island's heart and soul. Each piece of art, whether a beaded masterpiece or a vibrant painting, tells a narrative, communicating the essence of Curaçao's history, culture, and objectives. As I investigated the world of Curaçaoan creativity, I discovered that the island's arts and crafts are a palette of inspiration, enabling all who encounter them to connect with the beauty, distinctiveness, and authenticity that distinguish this unique Caribbean paradise.

The Vibrant Rhythms of Life in Curaçao.

When I first visited Curaçao's sun-drenched streets, I realized that the island's vivacious character comes to life during its festivals and celebrations. Curaçao's festivals, from the rhythmic pulses of traditional music to the explosion of colors that fill the air, are a dynamic expression of its cultural legacy and a tribute to the island's enthusiasm for life.

The Curaçao North Sea Jazz Festival is a jazz festival held annually on the Caribbean island of Curaçao. It brings together world-class performers and jazz fans for a vibrant musical festival. The festival features performances by globally famous performers in a variety of genres, including jazz, blues, soul, Latin, and pop. The festival is held in late August each year, attracting music fans from all over the world to experience a dynamic atmosphere and great live performances set against the background of Curaçao's tropical splendor.

Curaçao's Dia di Bandera, or Flag Day, is a prominent event devoted to the island's flag. Every year on July 2nd, the event celebrates the day in 1984 when the flag was first flown, indicating the island's constitutional autonomy within the Kingdom of the Netherlands. Parades, cultural exhibits, traditional music, and exhibitions are among the events, which provide a colorful representation of Curaçao's national pride and identity. It is a day when inhabitants gather together to commemorate their heritage and the island's unique position.

Curaçao celebrates Se, a traditional Afro-Caribbean harvest celebration. This boisterous and bright celebration is traditionally held on the island during the Easter season. The festival of Se is profoundly anchored in the island's history and African heritage, with colorful parades, traditional music, dancing, and ornate costumes. The event is a vibrant celebration of Curaçao's cultural variety, with participants performing rhythmic dances to the accompaniment of drums and other traditional instruments. It is an important cultural festival that brings communities together to remember their ancestors and celebrate their distinct identity.

Simadan is a traditional harvest celebration observed on the Caribbean island of Curaçao. It usually happens in February and March. The celebration celebrates the conclusion of the harvest season and has profound agricultural origins. During Simadan, people gather to harvest crops such as sugarcane and celebrate with vibrant festivals. Music, dancing, traditional costumes, and the production of local cuisine are all part of the celebration. It's a lively and culturally important festival that celebrates the island's agricultural past.

Marcha di Despedida, popularly known as the Farewell March, is a major cultural event held in Curaçao during the Carnival season. It commemorates the end of the Carnival celebrations and serves as a symbolic goodbye to the festive festivities. Participants march through the streets, decked in vivid costumes and accompanied by energetic music, creating a dynamic and enthusiastic scene. The march usually includes ornate floats, traditional music, and dance acts, and it serves as a pleasant and memorable end to the Carnival season in Curaçao.

The Tumba event is an annual music event held in Curaçao that showcases Tumba, one of the island's most distinctive music genres. Tumba is a colorful and rhythmic music distinguished by addictive rhythms and vivid tunes. Typically held around the Carnival season, the event serves as a platform for local singers and artists to participate in the Tumba music competition. Participants compose creative works that often focus on social and cultural concerns. The Tumba Festival is a dynamic celebration of Curaçao's musical legacy, attracting both residents and tourists to relish the lively and celebratory environment.

Curaçao's Bon Bini Festival is a colorful cultural festival that welcomes tourists with open arms. "Bon Bini" means "welcome" in the native language of Papiamento. This monthly event, which takes place in Willemstad, celebrates the island's rich history via music, dancing, and traditional crafts. Visitors may enjoy lively folkloric performances, sample local delicacies, and engage with craftspeople. The event is a lively celebration of Curaçao's unique culture, with a genuine and friendly welcome extended to everybody.

The Bon Bini Festival celebrates Curaçao's traditions with bright costumes, rhythmic music, and interactive exhibits. It's a chance for both residents and tourists to gather together, partake in the island's cultural pride, and enjoy the wonderful hospitality that distinguishes Curaçao. It's held in the center of Willemstad. The Bon Bini Festival represents the essence of the island's varied and dynamic people, with exciting acts, delectable local foods, and a friendly environment.

Carnival in Curaçao is an energetic and colorful event that occurs in the weeks before Lent. It's a bustling festival with vivid parades, spectacular costumes, music, and street dance. Both participants and spectators enjoy the celebratory atmosphere, which includes traditional music genres like as Tumba and colorful events such as road marches and Grand Parades. Carnival is a cultural spectacle that celebrates the island's rich past, with each area adding its flavor to the celebrations.

Curaçao's Carnival is a lively mix of traditional traditions and contemporary fun. The celebrations often include beautiful floats, complex costumes, and a diverse range of music genres, ranging from traditional rhythms to current compositions. The Grand Parade, in which dancers, musicians, and spectators fill the streets, is the culmination of the event. Carnival is not only a time for cheerful celebration, but it also reflects the cultural richness and dynamic spirit of Curaçao.

Daily Life and Social Norms are the beating hearts of Curaçaoan society.

Exploring the fabric of daily life and social norms in Curaçao is like seeing into the island's heart. The vibrant pulse of everyday life is a lovely dance of traditions, relationships, and ideals that weave the fabric of Curaçaoan society. As I immersed myself in the ebb and flow of daily life, I found the unique nuances that contribute to the island's uniqueness.

Genuine Relationships and Warm Greetings:
From the moment I walked in, I was greeted with warm smiles and respectful "bon bini" greetings. Curaçaoans take pride in their hospitality, and there is a strong sense of belonging. Walking around the markets, stopping at a local shop, or just walking down the street, the genuine connections I formed with locals reflected the island's welcoming nature and its people's want to share their culture.

Multiple Language Harmony:
Curaçao's linguistic diversity reflects the island's diverse history. While Dutch is the official language, English and Papiamento are widely used, creating a multilingual

symphony in everyday conversations. I was struck by how fast inhabitants switched between languages, a testament to the island's multiculturalism and ability to transcend cultural divides.

Sista, Embracing a Tranquil Moment:
In the middle of the day, I followed the habit of sista, a preferred time for rest and leisure. During this tranquil time, the bustling streets seemed to slow down, and I felt the island sigh as residents fled indoors or huddled under the shade of trees. The appreciation I got for taking a break from the day's activities reminded me of the importance of savoring life's modest pleasures.

A Taste of Heaven: Market Days
Curaçao's marketplaces were a sensory overload, with vibrant colors, great aromas, and lively conversation. On market days, locals and visitors engaged as they explored kiosks loaded with fresh vegetables, artisan crafts, and delectable street food. I enjoyed the opportunity to interact with sellers, sample local food, and become a part of the vibrant tapestry that is market life.

Elders and tradition must be respected:
Curaçaoan society is based mainly on elder respect and the preservation of cultural traditions. I saw how stories were passed down from generation to generation and rituals were maintained. Elders are revered for their knowledge, and their counsel is sought in both personal and communal matters. This intergenerational

argument highlights the island's will to preserve its unique customs.

Gatherings and Celebrations:
Curaçaoans like celebrating life's milestones and joys. Music, dancing, and pleasure fill the calendars of family reunions, municipal festivals, and religious meetings. I had the privilege of attending these gatherings, where I felt a tremendous sense of belonging and gratitude for the shared experiences that make life lovely.

Conclusion: A Symphony of Cultural Connections.
Curaçao's daily life and social rituals are a symphony of culture, connection, and community. As I accepted the island's rhythm, I discovered a way of life that honors tradition while embracing change, that celebrates diversity while fostering cooperation. Every touch, ritual, and aspect of daily life embodied the essence of Curaçaoan society - a culture woven with love, inclusivity, and a profound regard for life's richness.

Religion and spirituality

Curaçao's Religion and Spirituality: The Soul's Journey.

Curaçao's spiritual atmosphere is as diverse and fascinating as its natural beauty, weaving a tapestry of beliefs, rituals, and holy sites that give insight into the island's soul. In Curaçao, I embarked on a religious and spiritual journey that took me through ancient traditions, present practices, and the profound link between the spiritual and the ordinary.

A Religious Tapestry of Diversity.
The religious landscape of Curaçao is a patchwork of faiths brought to the island by the island's diverse demographics. Curaçao is a harmonious mix of religions that coexist and complement one another, ranging from Roman Catholicism, which flourished during colonial times, to Protestant denominations that followed, and from the Jewish population, which has thrived for generations, to recent arrivals such as Islam and Buddhism.

Faith's Historical Achievements:
Exploring Curaçao's historical landmarks gave me a greater perspective on the island's spiritual journey. The Mikvé Israel-Emanuel Synagogue, built in the 17th century, is a testament to the tenacity of Curaçao's Jewish population. The Fort Church (Fortkerk) displays the Christian influence, while the Mosque Al Hidaya serves as a religious venue for Curaçao's Muslim population. These buildings are more than just religious architecture; they are living monuments to bravery and endurance.

Festivals and Spiritual Traditions:
Participating in Curaçao's spiritual festivals allowed me to see the devotion and passion that define the island's culture. During the Corpus Christi Feast, I was drawn to the beautiful street carpets (sarchi) made of colored

sand and sawdust that served as a visual representation of religious devotion and artistic expression. The Dia di San Juan, which commemorated Saint John the Baptist, was a joyful event filled with bonfires, music, and cross-religious social activities.

Corpus Christi Feast (June) and Dia di San Juan (June 24th) are the dates.

Spirituality in Nature:
Curaçao's spirituality extends beyond religious institutions, blending with the natural environment. The island's allure, from its magnificent beaches to its peaceful coves, seemed to encourage reflection and meditation. As I stood on the edge of a cliff, looking out over the vast ocean, I felt a spiritual affinity with the natural forces that mirrored the beliefs of the indigenous people who had previously called this island home.

Contemporary Faith Expressions:
Spirituality manifests itself in a variety of ways in modern Curaçao, reflecting the island's colorful culture. Yoga retreats, health centers, and meditation sessions provide a space for individuals to connect with their inner selves and find peace amid the stresses of regular life. The blend of traditional wisdom and current practices highlights the island's attention to general well-being.

Finally, a Spiritual Journey.

Curaçao's journey into religion and spirituality is a soul journey that spans millennia of history, the rhythm of daily life, and the hallowed echoes of the natural environment. The island's spiritual environment, from ancient traditions to current expressions, is a testament to its capacity for cooperation, respect, and the ongoing quest for meaning. As I lost myself in Curaçao's spiritual tapestry, I felt a profound connection to the global strands that unite us all in our shared desire for the holy.

Willemstad is a thriving and varied city.

As I wandered inside Willemstad's happy embrace, I found myself wrapped in a living masterpiece of history, culture, and architectural grandeur. I discovered as I strolled along its cobblestone streets that Curaçao's capital city is more than simply a tourist attraction; it's a tapestry of colors, cultures, and experiences that embody the soul of the island's character.

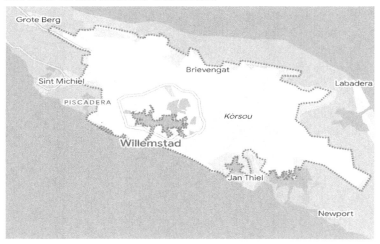

A Tale of Two Worlds: Punda and Otrobanda.
Willemstad is a city of contrasts, as the districts of Punda and Otrobanda beautifully demonstrate. I took the historic Queen Emma Bridge from the congested neighborhoods of Punda to the quiet beauty of

Otrobanda. Punda's pastel-colored homes attracted with its Dutch colonial grandeur, whilst Otrobanda's lanes had a more bohemian atmosphere, with art galleries and little stores putting a new twist on the historical tale.

Punda is in Willemstad, Curaçao.
Otrobanda is based in Willemstad, Curaçao.

On a Floating Market, authenticity reigns supreme.
My investigation took me to the Floating Market, a one-of-a-kind sensory experience in which boats from Venezuela deliver fresh fruits, vegetables, and seafood to the beaches of Willemstad. The brilliant colors of the market booths reflected the colors of the surrounding buildings, creating a visually appealing symphony. I found the genuine friendliness and cultural interchange that define everyday life in Willemstad via contacts with local businesses.

Sha Caprileskade is in Curacao's Willemstad.

Historical Landmarks: A Journey Through Time.
Willemstad is a living history museum, with UNESCO-listed architectural marvels transporting tourists back in time in its historic heart. Fort Amsterdam, perched on a hill above the city, provided breathtaking views of the river and its environs. The Fort Church (Fortkerk) is a testimony to the impact of Dutch colonialism, with its grand façade standing out against the blue Caribbean sky.
Curaçao, Willemstad, Handelskade.

The Mikvé Israel-Emanuel Synagogue is designated as a National Historic Landmark.
During my journey to Willemstad, I visited the Mikvé Israel-Emanuel Synagogue, the Western Hemisphere's

oldest continuously running synagogue. I felt a huge feeling of awe for the history and religion that had been maintained inside its walls as I stood before its stately facade and entered its sacred interiors. The Mikvé Israel-Emanuel Synagogue is a living tribute to Curaçao's Jewish community's perseverance and prosperity.

Willemstad, Curaçao (Heerenstraat).

Culinary Delights with Street Art: A Flavor and Creativity Fusion.

Willemstad is a sensory feast for the eyes and the mouth. The streets are covered with bright murals and street art, each brushstroke expressing a narrative about the essence of the city. The charming alleys lead to secret cafés and restaurants where I dined on both local and foreign food. Willemstad's gastronomic culture reflected the city's diverse and harmonious character, with its balance of flavor and ingenuity.

The concert finishes with Willemstad's Captivating Symphony.

Willemstad is more than capital; it's a symphony of colors, cultures, and experiences that enchants every visitor who wanders its picturesque streets. Every move, every structure, and every gathering tells something about the history, present, and future of Curaçao. Willemstad's vivid atmosphere lingered with me as I departed, a kaleidoscope of charm that imprinted itself on my heart and memories.

Willemstad is an enthralling tapestry that weaves together Curaçao's history, culture, and colorful personality. Every direction I turned, every structure I admired, and every contact I had with the residents showed a different facet of the city's personality. As I said Willemstad farewell, I carried not just memories of a place, but also a deep appreciation for the confluence of colors, cultures, and experiences that marks this lovely Caribbean treasure.

Beaches, Caves, and Other Natural Attractions

Beaches

Playa Knip, on Curaçao's western coast, is known for its breathtaking natural beauty. This gorgeous beach, located near the municipality of Westpunt, captivates tourists with its powdery white beaches and crystal-clear blue seas. Playa Knip is great for individuals looking for leisure, sunbathing, and immersing themselves in nature.

The beach provides a peaceful retreat, flanked by low cliffs and lush green hills. Its calm waters are ideal for swimming and snorkeling, allowing visitors to see the colorful marine life under the surface. Playa Knip is also a popular destination for both residents and visitors, attracting individuals who value natural beauty and a tranquil ambiance.

Cas Abao Beach is a beautiful white-sand beach on Curaçao's northwest coast, famed for its crystal-clear blue seas and spectacular coral reefs. This beach, located near the town of Cas Abao, has a gorgeous setting surrounded by lush green hills.

The beach is a popular location for water lovers, offering good snorkeling and diving chances among beautiful coral formations and rich aquatic life. Swimming and other water sports are perfect due to the quiet and welcoming seas. Visitors may also enjoy local drinks at the seaside bar and restaurant while relaxing on the gentle beaches. Cas Abao Beach's picturesque beauty and peacefulness make it a must-see destination for anyone looking for a relaxing day by the sea.

Grote Knip, also known as Playa Kenepa Grandi, is a beautiful beach on Curaçao's western coast. Grote Knip is a popular location for both residents and visitors, because of its stunning blue seas and powdery white sand. It is close to the settlement of Lagun.

The beach has a calm and pleasant ambiance, making it perfect for sunbathing and admiring the natural beauty of the Caribbean. Grote Knip's quiet and clear waters are ideal for swimming and snorkeling, letting tourists enjoy the diverse marine life close to the coast. Furthermore, the cliffs around the beach provide breathtaking views of the coastline, adding to the attractiveness of this scenic spot.

Playa Porto Mari: Located on Curaçao's west coast, Playa Porto Mari is a beautiful beach known for its white coral sand and crystal-clear blue seas. The beach is set in a quiet harbor, providing snorkelers and divers with a calm respite as well as a vivid underwater environment. Visitors may explore the bright coral reefs close off the coast, which are home to a diverse range of aquatic species. The beach has sunbathing opportunities, and the double reef offers calm swimming waters. Playa Porto Mari is more than simply a beach; it's a place for individuals looking for leisure as well as aquatic activities amid Curaçao's natural beauty.

Aside from its magnificent underwater surroundings, Playa Porto Mari offers guests to participate in a variety of aquatic sports. Snorkelers may find the abundant marine life only feet from the beach, while divers can journey further into the depths to study the complex intricacies of the reef. The beach also rents paddleboarding and kayaking equipment, giving a more tranquil approach to enjoy the coastal vistas. Playa Porto Mari, with its beautiful surroundings and a broad choice of aquatic activities, is a must-see for visitors looking for both peace and underwater thrills in Curaçao.

Kenepa Chiki, commonly known as Little Knip, is a beautiful beach on Curaçao's western coast. It's close to its more well-known neighbor, Playa Knip. The beach is recognized for its pure white sand, crystal-clear blue waves, and rich flora that surrounds it.

For guests seeking a more relaxing beach experience, Kenepa Chiki provides a calm and attractive location. It's a great place for swimming, snorkeling, and just resting on the smooth sands while admiring the stunning views of the Caribbean Sea. The tranquil seas make it ideal for a variety of water sports, offering the ideal setting for a relaxing day by the sea.

Playa Lagun is a beautiful beach situated in a cove between two cliffs on Curaçao's northwest coast. This beach, located near the town of Laguna, is well-known for its quiet ambiance and crystal-clear waves. It's surrounded by thick foliage, making for a beautiful background.

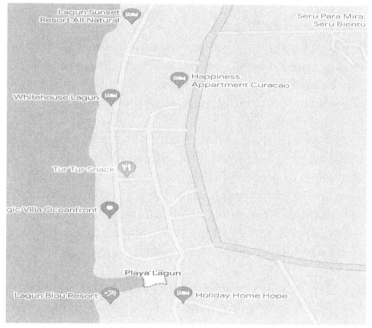

Because of its abundant marine life and coral structures, the beach is a popular snorkeling and diving destination. Snorkelers and divers may explore the underwater world, where they may see colorful fish, coral reefs, and even marine turtles. The tranquil, blue waters are great for aquatic sports, while the nearby cliffs provide options for cliff jumping or just taking in the scenery.

Playa Lagun is less congested than some of the bigger beaches, making it a more tranquil experience for those looking for a relaxing day by the sea. It's a hidden treasure for nature lovers and water aficionados, offering the ideal combination of leisure and underwater exploration.

Blue Bay Beach, on Curaçao's southern coast, is famous for its gorgeous white sand and crystal-clear blue seas. This beautiful beach provides a tranquil respite and is well-known for its family-friendly vibe.

Blue Bay Beach's water activities are diversified, appealing to a wide range of interests. Visitors may go snorkeling to see the beautiful marine life right off the coast, or they can try their hand at paddleboarding while enjoying the tranquil Caribbean seas. The beach is well-equipped for kayaking, allowing both novices and expert paddlers to enjoy the coastal beauty.

Blue Bay Beach, with its gently sloping sandy beach, is also great for swimming and provides a safe atmosphere for families. Sunbathers may unwind on the gentle beaches while admiring the stunning views of the Caribbean Sea. Blue Bay is a popular location for individuals seeking both leisure and aquatic adventures due to the beach's accessibility and the variety of water sports offered.

Caves

Hato Caves, near Willemstad on Curaçao's northern tip, is a remarkable natural site with historical and geological importance. Nature built out these limestone caverns with stunning stalactites, stalagmites, and unique formations over millennia.

Visitors to Hato Caves may take guided tours that dive into the site's geological characteristics and cultural history. The experienced guides tell stories about the cave's history, including its usage as a hideout for runaway slaves. The tour gives an immersive experience, showing the cave's mesmerizing beauty while recounting its unique history.

Furthermore, the cave system supports a rich ecology that includes bats and other cave-adapted species. Exploring Hato Caves combines excitement, knowledge, and an intimate experience with the natural beauties that lie under Curaçao's surface.

Boca Tabla Cave is an enthralling natural marvel found inside Shete Boka National Park on Curaçao's northern shore. This seaside cave is famous for its spectacular sea views and the intense ocean pressures that cut distinctive shapes into the rocks. The constant waves smashing into the cave provide a stunning show of natural forces for visitors to Boca Tabla. The site is not only beautiful, but it also provides chances for coastal treks and exploration of Shete Boka National Park's rough, gorgeous landscapes.

Playa Hundu Cave is a stunning natural marvel found in Curaçao's western region. This cave near Playa Hundu Beach provides a one-of-a-kind and relatively secret exploring opportunity. Visitors may go cave exploring, marveling at the fascinating rock formations, and relaxing in the tranquil ambiance. The cave is an extension of the island's diversified nature, offering visitors looking for adventure the opportunity to explore a lesser-known nevertheless intriguing element of Curaçao's natural splendor.

Playa Grandi Cave is a beautiful natural feature in Playa Grandi, a beach famed for its pure waters and abundance of marine life. The cave is located on the island's western side and provides tourists with a unique chance to explore the island's natural treasures. The surroundings, which include harsh coastal vistas and spectacular cliffs, provide a stunning background for the cave.

Scenic walks are popular activities around Playa Grandi Cave, which is typically accessible by coastal paths. Explorers may marvel at the cave's unique rock formations and take in panoramic views of the Caribbean Sea. The location is also popular with adventure seekers and nature lovers who enjoy the peace and serenity of the remote seaside surroundings. It's great for anyone wishing to get away from the hustle and bustle of the city and immerse themselves in Curaçao's natural beauties.

Shete Boka National Park, situated on Curaçao's northern coast, is known for its rough and dramatic scenery, as well as enticing caverns. These caverns, carved by the sea's unrelenting power, are among the park's distinctive geological structures. Visitors may explore these seaside caverns and marvel at nature's unique designs. Shete Boka National Park provides a beautiful view of tremendous waves slamming against the rocks. Cave exploration, hiking routes, and seeing the awe-inspiring phenomenon of the "Boka Tabla," where waves slam into an underground cavern, producing a fascinating show, are among the activities available in the park.

Playa Lagun Cave lies near Playa Lagun, a beautiful beach on Curaçao's northwest coast. This cave is tucked along the rocky beach, giving a fascinating addition to the surrounding natural splendor. Visitors to Playa Lagun often visit the cave, marveling at its unusual geological structures.

Beachcombing along Playa Lagun, snorkeling in the clean seas to find marine life, and relaxing in the tranquil coastal settings are all activities near Playa Lagun Cave. The cave itself provides a chance for some exploring as well as a cool respite from the sun. The charm of the beach, the cave, and the surrounding natural environment combine to offer Playa Lagun a calm and intriguing site for tourists to relax and enjoy Curaçao's coastal beauties.

Other attractions include:

Christoffel National Park is the island's biggest national park and is located on the island's northwest side. It includes the steep Christoffel Mountain, Curaçao's highest point, which provides stunning panoramic views of the island. Hiking, bird viewing, and animal observation are among the activities available to park visitors. The park's flora and animals are diversified, including rare orchids and the local white-tailed deer. The daring may attempt the difficult trek to the peak of Christoffel Mountain, while others may opt to explore the park's well-marked paths, which lead to breathtaking landscapes and historic monuments.

Shete Boka National Park is situated on Curaçao's rough and scenic northern coast. This coastal park is famous for its spectacular vistas, sea caves, and the Caribbean Sea's powerful waves breaking against the limestone cliffs. Visitors to the park may explore various bays, each with its distinctive vistas and opportunity to see the force of the ocean. Hiking along well-marked routes, seeing numerous bird species, and watching sea turtles breeding are all popular pastimes. The park offers an enthralling combination of environment, animals, and the raw beauty of the sea.

Klein Curaçao, or "Little Curaçao," is a tiny, deserted island approximately 6 miles southeast of Curaçao. It is famous for its gorgeous white sand beaches and turquoise seas. Klein Curaçao activities often include snorkeling to explore vivid coral reefs, swimming with sea turtles, sunning on isolated beaches, and learning about the island's historic lighthouse. The excursion to Klein Curaçao often includes a boat ride, which allows guests to appreciate the gorgeous views of the Caribbean Sea.

Hiking Mount Christoffel in Curaçao is an exciting outdoor excursion. This climb travels to Mount Christoffel, the island's highest peak, and is located in Christoffel National Park on the western side of the island. The walk offers breathtaking panoramic views of the surrounding regions, including the northern and southern beaches.

The trek is a popular pastime for nature lovers since it allows them to experience the national park's unique flora and animals. The trip to the peak is a relatively difficult walk but is rewarded with beautiful sights that make the effort worthwhile. You may come across indigenous vegetation, bird species, and other animals along the journey.

Aside from the main path to Mount Christoffel, the national park has numerous trails for shorter treks and exploration. The region is densely forested, making it an ideal location for individuals seeking a connection with nature. Hiking Mount Christoffel provides a remarkable and exhilarating experience amid Curaçao's natural splendor, whether you're an enthusiastic hiker or a casual nature lover.

The Flamingo Sanctuary in Jan Kok is a gorgeous site on Curaçao's island where tourists may marvel at the elegant elegance of these unique pink birds. The sanctuary, which is located near the salt pans on the island's west coast, offers a natural home for flamingos and is a paradise for birdwatchers and environment aficionados. Visitors may see these graceful birds in their natural habitat, frequently taking magnificent images of the flamingos against the background of the salt flats and the Caribbean Sea. The sanctuary has a tranquil environment that makes it suitable for a calm walk or silent contemplation of the natural surroundings.

Landhuis Kenepa is a historical plantation home that has been converted into a museum in the western section of Curaçao. This cultural treasure provides tourists with an insight into the island's history and participation in the transatlantic slave trade. Exhibits at the museum include the history of the plantation, the life of enslaved people, and Curaçao's cultural heritage.

Visitors to Landhuis Kenepa may tour the plantation house's well-preserved chambers, which display antiques, pictures, and papers from various eras. The experienced team gives insights into the island's and its people's complicated history.

Furthermore, Landhuis Kenepa often conducts cultural events, seminars, and educational activities that enhance the visiting experience. The plantation's beautiful grounds provide a quiet background, providing a contemplative setting for individuals interested in Curaçao's historical and cultural legacy.

Forts, museums, and architecture are examples of historic landmarks.

Fort Amsterdam is a historic fortification in Willemstad, Curaçao, with origins reaching back to the 17th century. It was built in 1635 by the Dutch as a military outpost to safeguard the precious natural harbor of St. Anna Bay from prospective attackers.

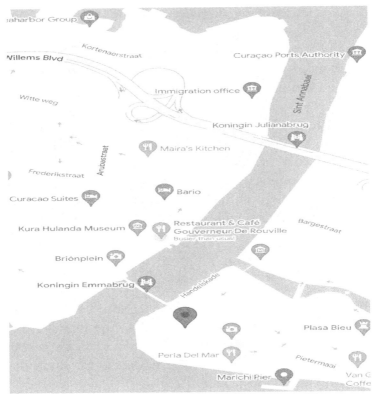

Today, Fort Amsterdam is a reminder of the island's colonial heritage and serves as the headquarters of Curaçao's government. The fort's architectural characteristics, such as high walls and guns, represent the military architecture of the period. The internal courtyard has been converted into a public plaza, and the surrounding area houses government offices, stores, and cultural activities.

Visitors to Fort Amsterdam may learn about its history, enjoy breathtaking views of Willemstad, and admire the combination of colonial architecture and modern functionality. The fort is an important landmark in the middle of the capital city and plays an important part in Curaçao's history.

Fort Nassau is a medieval fort on the island of Curaçao that rises on a hill overlooking the city, of Willemstad. Originally built by the Dutch in the 18th century, the fort has fulfilled a variety of functions throughout its history, including military defense and signaling.

Fort Nassau has been converted into a restaurant with spectacular views of the island. Visitors may tour the grounds of the fort, take in the historical atmosphere, and dine while taking in beautiful views of Willemstad, the surrounding ocean, and the colorful island scenery. The fort embodies both Curaçao's colonial past and its adaptation to modern usage, making it a one-of-a-kind attraction for history buffs and visitors looking for a lovely location for eating and leisure.

Rif Fort is a medieval stronghold in Willemstad, Curaçao, that has been transformed into a busy commercial and entertainment complex. Rif Fort, which was built in the 1820s to guard the entrance to St. Anna Bay, has undergone substantial repairs and is now a famous tourist site. The fort's architectural splendor has been maintained, and tourists may explore a variety of stores, restaurants, and cafés inside its walls. The scenic setting provides breathtaking views of the Caribbean Sea, combining the historical value of the fort with a modern and energetic ambiance. Rif Fort exemplifies Curaçao's ability to smoothly merge its rich past with contemporary conveniences.

Kura Hulanda Museum in Willemstad, Curaçao, is an enthralling museum that explores the history of the transatlantic slave trade and the African diaspora. The museum is housed in a beautifully renovated complex of 19th-century buildings and has a large collection of antiques, displays, and multimedia presentations.

Visitors to the Kura Hulanda Museum may learn about the traumatic voyage of enslaved Africans, the hardships of the Middle Passage, and the effect of slavery on the Caribbean. The museum also has exhibitions on African civilizations, emphasizing African peoples' perseverance, contributions, and rich legacy.

The museum is well-known for its thought-provoking displays, which include life-sized sculptures and realistic renderings that give a moving and immersive experience. Kura Hulanda Museum is a valuable educational resource that sheds light on the difficult history of slavery while encouraging conversation and understanding.

The Curaçao Marine Museum, located in Willemstad's historic waterfront sector, is an enthralling institution that dives into the island's marine history. The museum, housed in the magnificent estate of the Van den Brandhof family, shows relics, exhibits, and interactive displays that tell the narrative of Curaçao's connection with the sea.

The Nautical Museum allows visitors to learn about numerous facets of nautical life, such as the island's function as a busy port, its naval history, and the importance of shipping in the Caribbean. The museum also has a broad collection of model ships, nautical devices, and shipwreck items.

The Maritime Museum's strategic position overlooking St. Anna Bay gives a lovely backdrop that compliments the rich heritage it maintains. Whether you're interested in sailing exploits or the economic and cultural consequences of maritime operations, this museum will take you on a fascinating tour through Curaçao's maritime past.

The Curaçao Museum, located in Otrobanda, Willemstad, is a cultural institution that provides an in-depth look at the island's history, art, and culture. The museum's displays cover many centuries, showing objects, papers, and artworks that illustrate Curaçao's unique legacy. It is housed in a beautifully restored colonial-era structure.

The Curaçao Museum allows visitors to immerse themselves in the island's history, from its indigenous beginnings to the colonial period and beyond. The exhibits of the museum address topics such as the slave trade, local customs, and the effect of many civilizations on Curaçao. It offers a more nuanced knowledge of the island's development, making it an important cultural and educational center.

The museum's central position makes it readily accessible, and guided tours are provided for anyone interested in a more in-depth examination. The Curaçao Museum is a captivating place for a greater awareness of the island's legacy, whether you're interested in historical relics, creative manifestations, or the rich tapestry of Curaçao's cultural narrative.

The Queen Emma Pontoon Bridge is a historic and famous feature in Curaçao's capital, Willemstad. This floating bridge, often known as the "Swinging Old Lady," joins the Punda and Otrobanda neighborhoods over St. Anna Bay. Its distinctive design distinguishes it: the bridge is hinged and swings out horizontally to let ships pass through the harbor.

This pedestrian bridge is an important feature of Willemstad's appeal, providing spectacular views of the colorful waterfront buildings and contributing to the city's lively atmosphere. The Queen Emma Pontoon Bridge, one of the city's oldest and most distinctive elements, is not only a method of crossing the bay but also a symbol of Curaçao's rich nautical history and architectural legacy.

Pietermaai District is a historic area in Willemstad, Curaçao, known for its colorful and well-renovated houses. Pietermaai, formerly a lively residential district for wealthy Dutch merchants, fell into ruin but has recently undergone major restoration.

The neighborhood has a fascinating mix of architectural styles, with colonial Dutch and Caribbean influences. Visitors may enjoy a vivid assortment of pastel-colored façades, fashionable boutique hotels, art galleries, and a broad choice of restaurants and cafés while strolling along its tiny lanes.

Pietermaai is not just a visual treat, but also a cultural hotspot. The area is a vibrant and energetic portion of Willemstad, hosting a variety of cultural events, live music performances, and art exhibits. It has evolved into a fashionable and bohemian district while keeping its historic beauty, drawing both residents and visitors looking for a unique combination of history and modern culture.

The Mikvé Israel-Emanuel Synagogue in Willemstad, Curaçao, is one of the Americas' oldest synagogues still in existence. It is a UNESCO World Heritage monument and a prominent emblem of the island's rich cultural past, having been built in 1732.

The synagogue is built in a mix of architectural styles that represent both Sephardic and Ashkenazi influences. It has sand flooring, metal candelabras, and an outstanding collection of religious items. The neighboring Jewish Cultural Historical Museum explores the Jewish community's contributions to Curaçao over the ages.

Mikvé Israel-Emanuel Synagogue is a monument to the island's religious tolerance legacy since the Jewish population has prospered alongside other cultural and religious groups. Visitors may visit the synagogue's ancient sanctuary and obtain a better knowledge of Curaçao's unique past.

The Pontjesbrug, commonly known as the Queen Emma Bridge, is a floating pedestrian bridge in Willemstad, Curaçao's capital. This magnificent bridge spans the entrance to St. Anna Bay and links the Punda and Otrobanda neighborhoods. Its unusual structure - the bridge is hinged and opens to enable marine traffic to pass across - distinguishes it.

The Queen Emma Bridge swings up and closes on massive pontoons, providing a sight for residents and tourists alike. When the bridge is open, a free boat service known as 'Marshe Bieuw,' takes people over the bay. Pontjesbrug's brilliant colors and lively ambiance make it a favorite destination for both daytime strolls and nighttime parties, with stunning views of Willemstad's historic shoreline.

Curaçao's Charming Villages: A Tapestry of Local Encounters.

Beyond the well-trodden streets of Curaçao's busy center, I set out on an exploring journey through its lovely villages. These hidden treasures revealed a real world in which the rhythms of local life and the warmth of genuine relationships weave a magnificent tapestry of cultural immersion. Each community greeted me with open arms, allowing me to see the heart and spirit of the Curaçao people.

Scharloo: A Colorful Kaleidoscope
Scharloo Street, Willemstad, Curaçao

I was drawn to a site where vivid buildings produced a striking picture against the sky as I drove through Scharloo's little alleys. The old houses were a tribute to the island's unique heritage, with beautiful workmanship and a rainbow of colors. I felt a feeling of camaraderie and solidarity that transcended language and country as I met with people going about their everyday lives, reminding me of the strength of our humanity.

Barber: Peace amid Nature's splendor.
The site is Barber, Curaçao.

Barber greeted me with open arms, its tranquil surroundings a wonderful respite from the outside world's hurry and bustle. When I explored the hamlet, which was surrounded by beautiful terrain and rolling hills, I was amazed at the simplicity of life. During my interactions with the people, I learned their deep connection to the land and respect for nature. The serenity that surrounded me while I sat in the shadow of a tree couldn't help but inspire me.

Embracing Soto's Local Customs
The postal code for Curaçao is Soto.

Soto took us into the heart of Curaçao's rural life, where time appeared to flow at its speed. The villagers' devotion to preserving traditions and the strong feeling of community that dominated their interactions with me astounded me. I had the opportunity to participate in a local dance led by the beating of drums and the laughing of new acquaintances. I felt a strong connection to Hamlet and his inhabitants at the time as if I were a part of their continuous drama.

Santa Martha is a Sanctuary for Peace.
The postal code for Curaçao is Santa Martha.

Santa Martha, positioned between the sea and the mountains, offers a haven of peace and natural beauty. The settlement's closeness to the sea, as well as its picturesque surroundings, appeared to foster thought and meditation. I wandered for hours along the beach, feeling the sand between my toes and admiring the sun's golden rays on the ocean. Interacting with local fishermen provided me with insight into their way of life as well as the enormous respect they had for the sea's riches.

Bandabou: The Authenticity Rhythm.
Curaçao and Bandabou (the western side of the island)

While exploring the Bandabou villages, I stumbled into a spot where authenticity reigned supreme. I saw a kaleidoscope of local experiences that left an unforgettable imprint on my travels, from crowded marketplaces to calm countryside. When I chatted with artists, farmers, and storytellers, I sensed a bond that transcends cultural boundaries. The villages of Bandabou radiated real compassion, reminding me of the beauty that develops when strangers become friends.

Curaçao's lovely towns are more than simply tourist traps; they are entry points for real encounters, passionate connections, and the pulsing pulse of local life. Each town provided a distinct viewpoint, providing a look into the island's eclectic cultural mix. As I strolled the cobblestone streets, laughed with locals, and marveled at nature's splendor, I knew that these were not transitory moments, but threads that would weave themselves into the fabric of my tale, eternally linking me to the spirit of Curaçao.
Insider Advice for the Perfect Vacation

To thoroughly immerse myself in the vivid tapestry of Curaçaoan culture, I researched local customs and traditions. I encountered a world of gestures, customs, and social conventions as I interacted with the island's kind and welcoming population, which formed a vivid image of Curaçao's culture and values.

The greeting "Bon Bini" means "Warm Welcome."
The term "Bon bini" translates to "welcome" and is more than simply a greeting; it signifies the island's hospitality and the real warmth of its inhabitants. "Bon bini" was a worldwide welcome that cut over language boundaries and quickly put me at ease, whether I was entering a business, meeting a new friend, or exploring a local area.

Elder respect is a time-honored practice.
In Curaçaoan culture, elder reverence is highly valued. I saw how younger generations connected with their elders, whether by greeting them or conversing with them. This ritual highlighted the island's importance of knowledge, tradition transmission, and generational connectivity.

A Melody in Several Languages.
Curaçao, a Dutch Caribbean island, is well-known for its language variety, which represents the island's cosmopolitan background. Even though Dutch is the official language, Papiamento, a unique Creole mix, is widely spoken and understood. English and Spanish are

also widely spoken, resulting in a linguistic symphony that reflects the island's cosmopolitanism and flexibility.

Dressing modestly and culturally sensitively.

When visiting holy places or interacting with people, I became aware of the need for modest clothes. While the island has a laid-back vibe, dressing appropriately is a cultural statement. It's a method of expressing gratitude for the traditions and principles that are strongly embedded in Curaçaoan culture.

Personal Space and Interaction: A Balance of Warmth and Respect.

I witnessed a great blend of kindness and respect for personal space in my contacts with locals. Handshakes and embraces were heartily shared, showing the island's friendly nature. However, I saw a huge regard for limits, as shown by gestures and talks that were steeped in decorum and mutual respect.

Dining Etiquette for Special Occasions.

Lunch with locals was an excellent chance to learn about Curaçaoan eating customs. Mealtime became more than simply a source of nourishment for me; it became a treasured occasion for connection and bonding. Breaking bread became a strong symbol of connection and camaraderie as the delicacies of the island were shared.

Festivals & Celebrations: Spreading Joy.

Participating in Curaçao's bright holidays and festivities exposed me to practices that promote community pleasure firsthand. From vibrant street parades to religious processions, each event underscored the island's love of celebration, music, dancing, and inclusion. Participating in these festivals enabled me to tap into the communal spirit and immerse myself in the cultural pulse of Curaçao.

Cultural harmony and shared ideas exist.
Curaçao's traditions and etiquette exemplify the island's tranquility, solidarity, and tolerance for variety. As I negotiated these social traditions, I saw how they were woven into the fabric of daily life, joining individuals of many generations and cultures. Whether it was a friendly "Bon bini," a kind gesture, or a shared meal, I learned that these rituals were more than just rituals; they were bridges that linked hearts, creating a feeling of belonging and understanding that spanned borders and formed a common sense of identity.
Information on Health and Safety

Information about health and safety for a safe vacation to Curacao.

A terrific Curaçao vacation requires not just a feeling of adventure, but also a dedication to safety and well-being. As you immerse yourself in the beauty and culture of the island, it's essential to prioritize your health and security to have a worry-free and enjoyable holiday. To help you make the most of your stay, below is a detailed list of safety and health recommendations:

Precautions for Health:

Immunizations: Check that your usual immunizations are up to date before traveling to Curaçao. Depending on your particular health and the nature of your journey, consider immunizations or preventive treatments for illnesses such as hepatitis A and typhoid.

Curaçao has excellent medical facilities and well-equipped hospitals. Find out where the closest medical facilities are to your hotel, particularly if you have unique medical requirements.

Prescription medications: Bring enough for the length of your stay if you depend on them. Carry a copy of your meds as well as a doctor's letter if required.

General Safety Recommendations:

Although Curaçao is typically safe, use care and common sense, particularly in tourist areas. Keep your stuff secure and avoid exhibiting precious goods.

Natural disasters: Be aware of the weather, particularly during hurricane season (June to November). Keep an eye out for any local government warnings or advisories.

Water Safety: Curaçao's waters are beautiful, but always use caution while swimming, snorkeling, or diving. Keep an eye out for local signs, listen to lifeguards' advice, and be mindful of currents.

Local laws and customs: Dress modestly and follow local laws and traditions while visiting holy places. Except in certain circumstances, public nudity is illegal.

Driving Safety: If you want to drive, be sure you have a valid license and follow all local traffic laws. Drive slowly, particularly on unknown routes, and don't go above the speed limit.

Emergency Phone Numbers: Learn the emergency phone numbers for your local police, medical services, and your country's embassy or consulate.

Food Safety and Water Quality:

While drinking tap water is normally safe, many tourists prefer bottled water. Consult locals or your hotel for the most up-to-date information.

Food Hygiene: Savor the gastronomic pleasures of Curaçao, but only from reputable restaurants and street sellers. Choose well-cooked meals, and peel fruits before eating.

Food allergies and dietary restrictions should be properly communicated to restaurant employees to offer a pleasant eating experience.

Insect Defense:

Mosquitoes: Use insect repellent, wear long sleeves and trousers, and sleep beneath mosquito nets if required to minimize mosquito-borne diseases.

Travel Warnings:

Stay up to date on travel warnings issued by your country's government or relevant health groups. Keep an eye out for changes before and throughout your travel so that you may make educated choices based on the most up-to-date information.

Curaçao provides an enticing mix of adventure and leisure, and you may completely immerse yourself in its allure by taking the appropriate safety and health measures. To guarantee that your trip is not only fun but also safe and secure, prepare wisely, educate yourself, and practice caution while exploring this wonderful region.

Eco-Friendly Travel Practice

Curaçao's Beauty for Future Generations: Practices for Sustainable Travel

As a responsible visitor, I saw the need to practice sustainable tourism in Curaçao to leave a positive legacy and protect the island's natural and cultural assets for future generations. I was able to mix my wanderlust with a true commitment to environmental and cultural preservation by making eco-conscious decisions and engaging in mindful activities.

Conservation Initiatives that Respect Nature's Balance

To preserve the fragile balance of Curaçao's ecosystems, sustainable travel is required. I made it a point to leave a modest trace in nature by following Leave No Trace principles and avoiding harming animals while hiking. I took part in scheduled conservation events including beach clean-ups and coral reef restoration programs, which helped to ensure the natural beauty of Curaçao's long-term health.

Increasing the Cultural Resilience of the Local Community.

Aside from environmental concerns, sustainable tourism on the island involves community support. I made it a point to stay at locally owned hotels, dine at family-run restaurants, and buy handcrafted items from craftsmen. Participating in guided excursions and cultural exchanges with locals not only broadened my experience but also developed my bonds with the Curaçaoans.

Ethical interactions with wildlife.

I kept a respectful distance from aquatic critters when snorkeling and diving to avoid upsetting their habitats or habits. I picked operators that emphasize animal care and ethical practices, according to recommendations for safe animal relationships. By protecting marine ecosystems, I helped to ensure the long-term survival of the wonderful creatures that make Curaçao's waters home.

Using eco-friendly transportation decreases your carbon impact.

I employed eco-friendly forms of transportation wherever feasible to lessen my environmental effects. I toured the surrounding places by using public transportation, walking, or renting bicycles, reducing my carbon footprint and enjoying the island at my speed. I was able to lessen air pollution and traffic congestion by adopting ecologically friendly transportation.

Reduced waste and energy use are examples of resource conservation.

I conserve water and energy at my lodgings by reusing towels and shutting off lights and air conditioning when not in use. To prevent single-use plastic waste, I carried a reusable water bottle and shopping bag, and I made an effort to promote businesses that use eco-friendly practices, such as limiting plastic packaging.

Education for Cultural Sensitivity.
I immersed myself in local culture by engaging in polite discussions, adopting local customs, and attempting to comprehend the beliefs and traditions of Curaçao's communities. I took informative tours and talks on the island's history, culture, and conservation initiatives, which deepened my connection to and respect for the place I was fortunate enough to visit.

My voyage across Curaçao was about becoming a responsible custodian of that beauty, rather than just finding it. By adopting sustainable travel practices, I left a lovely legacy for future generations by supporting the island's ecosystem, strengthening its people, and preserving its cultural traditions. I left Curaçao with not just recollections of stunning scenery, but also the pleasure of knowing that my feet had expressed a commitment to responsible travel and a shared responsibility to protect and love the earth we all share.

Lodging choices range from resorts to guesthouses.

Where Comfort Meets Variety.

Curaçao's numerous lodging possibilities appeal to all types of tourists, whether they desire opulent delight, true immersion, or cost-effective comfort. The island's hotel alternatives guarantee that each stay is unique and individualized, from opulent resorts that pamper the senses to tiny guest cottages that provide a look into local life.

Luxurious Resorts: An Exotic Oasis.

Curaçao's biggest resorts give a terrific vacation for anyone searching for elegance and relaxation. With magnificent beachfront settings, gigantic pools, world-class spas, and superb restaurants, these resorts offer a refuge of leisure and grandeur. From private pool cabanas to excellent culinary experiences, great service and attention to detail guarantee that every need is addressed. While costs vary widely depending on hotel style, time of year, and other facilities, a genuinely magnificent trip should cost between $300 and $800 per night.

Boutique Hotels Add Elegance and Charm.

Curaçao boutique hotels give individual attention, distinctive flair, and a feeling of location. These modest cottages are full of individuality and charm, and they typically embody the island's cultural heritage and creative flare. Boutique hotels give a more personal and immersive experience, with thoughtful facilities, exquisite décor, and an emphasis on establishing a feeling of community. Prices vary from $150 to $350 per night, giving a middle-of-the-road alternative that mixes quality and affordability.

Accepting Local Hospitality at Guesthouses and Bed & Breakfasts.

Visitors may discover Curaçao through the eyes of islanders by staying in guesthouses or bed & breakfasts. These lodgings, which are tucked among neighborhoods and communities, allow a real peek into island life. Warm hospitality, home-cooked meals, and personal encounters contribute to creating a home-away-from-home sense. Guesthouses and bed & breakfasts are an intriguing alternative for budget-conscious guests hoping for a comfortable and culturally rich experience, with costs ranging from $80 to $150 per night.

Create Your Own Home with Vacation Rentals and Apartments.

Vacation rentals and apartments offer a home-like setting in which travelers may develop their schedules and routines for people who appreciate flexibility and freedom. Fully equipped kitchens, vast living rooms, and the possibility to connect with locals all add to an immersive experience. Vacation rentals and apartments may cost between $100 and $300 a night, depending on size, location, and amenities, making them an intriguing choice for families and groups.

Eco-Lodges & Nature Retreats immerse you in nature's embrace.

Eco-lodges and nature retreats give a unique chance to connect with Curaçao's natural beauty while reducing environmental effects. These lodgings frequently blend well with their environment, allowing an inconspicuous getaway into nature. Eco-lodges, which promote sustainability and outdoor activities, give travelers an immersive experience that enables them to appreciate the nature of the island. The cost of an eco-friendly retreat varies, but it should cost between $150 and $250 a night.

Curaçao's hotel selections reflect the island's variety and offer a broad range of experiences to match any traveler's interests and budget. Whether indulging in luxury, partaking in local culture, or seeking a home away from home, the island's accommodations guarantee that every visit is an occasion to build treasured memories and experience the real spirit of Curaçao. It's vital to note that the costs provided are approximations and may change depending on a variety of variables, so it's better to check with individual hotels for the most up-to-date rates and availability.

How to Get Around: Transportation

Curaçao's well-connected transit alternatives appeal to a wide array of interests and pricing, making moving around a snap. From efficient public buses and rental vehicles to taxis and cycling, the island provides a choice of options to explore its bright landscape, little communities, and hidden gems.

Public transportation is both economical and readily accessible.

Each ride costs between $1 and $2.

Curaçao's public buses, known as "Konvooi," offer an economical and dependable method of transportation for those who wish to explore the island's major routes. These buses run on schedules and link major cities, tourist spots, and attractions. With rates ranging from $1 to $2 per journey, public buses are an inexpensive way to go around while also mingling with people and observing ordinary life on the island.

Renting a car enables you to embark on excursions.
The fee varies based on the style of the car and the duration of the rental term.

Curaçao vehicle rental allows you to explore the island at your speed. Rental firms give a broad selection of vehicles, from modest cars to SUVs, enabling you to venture off the usual route and uncover hidden pearls. Daily costs vary depending on the car model, rental period, and insurance coverage. A regular automobile rental would generally cost from $40 to $100 per day, with reductions available for extended rental periods.

Taxis are adaptable and convenient.
The pricing varies based on the distance and location.

Taxis in Curaçao offer rapid door-to-door service, making them a perfect solution for those wanting a stress-free journey. Taxi rates are not metered, so clarify the fare with the driver before starting. Short journeys within town may cost $10-20, while lengthier travels to outlying locations or attractions may cost $30-70. Sharing a cab with numerous people may assist in dividing the cost and make this alternative more cost-effective.

Cycling is an ecologically friendly adventure.
The pricing varies based on the rental period and location.

Exploring Curaçao by bike is both environmentally sensible and entertaining. Several rental firms offer bicycles, with rates ranging depending on the model and period of rental. On average, renting a bicycle costs between $15 and $25 per day. Cycling enables you to explore the island's landscapes and settlements at your leisure, connecting you with nature and the local culture.

Walking through Charm.
Many of Curaçao's cities, neighborhoods, and attractions may be accessed by foot. Walking enables you to discover the island's environment at your leisure, exploring secret passageways, tiny markets, and architectural marvels along the road. Strolling about Willemstad's colorful streets or visiting the peaceful countryside gives an intimate connection to the island's beauty and charm.

Discovering Your Ideal Career Path
Curaçao's transportation alternatives are wide enough to fit any traveler's interests and budget. Whether you

select the inexpensive cost of public transit, the freedom of a rental vehicle, the convenience of taxis, the eco-friendliness of cycling, or the personal discovery of walking, each means of transportation enables you to immerse yourself in the island's rich tapestry. Prices are estimations and may vary depending on variables such as location, period of stay, and individual preferences. Contact particular transport firms for the most up-to-date information on cost and availability.

Important Papiamento Phrases

Essential Papiamento Phrases for Connecting.

Adopting the local language, Papiamento, as a traveler in Curaçao helps communication while also exhibiting respect for the culture and improving your complete experience. While English is commonly spoken on the island, mastering a few basic words in Papiamento will help you to converse with people and immerse yourself in the lively culture.

Greetings and fundamental expressions:
• Good day - Bon dia
• Good afternoon - Ciao
• Good night/evening - Bon nochi
• Good day, afternoon, and evening - Hello, afternoon, and evening
• Ayo- Goodbye
• Thank you very much, Danki.
• Di nada - Thank you very much.
• Please, favor.

• What are your thoughts? - How are things going for you?

Common Protocol:
• Mi number ta...- My name is...
• My hometown is... - My name is...
• Mi ta komprondé - I don't comprehend.
• Mi por papia un poko di Papiamentu - I know a little Papiamento.

Fundamental Issues:
• Unda? - Where?
• Kon? - How?
• Kiko? - What?
• Ken? - Who?
• Is pa unda bo ta bai correct? - What are your intentions?

Food & Dining:
• Un kofi, por favor fabor - Please have a cup of coffee.
• Un awa - Water
• Mi ke... - I'd like to...
• Mi tin chamber - I'm hungry
• Mi ta alergiko pa...- I'm allergic to...

Directions:
Rigá - Straight
• Sinta robez - Turn left
• Make a right - Sinta drechi
• to - stop
• Un mapa, por favor - Could you kindly supply a map?

Numbers:
- 1 - un
- 2 - dos
- 3 - tres

quarter - 4 points
- 5 - sink
- 6 - sheet
- 7 - sheet
- 8 - Ocho
- 9- number
- 10 - dies

Time:

Orario - Orario
- Can you tell me what time it is?- Could you simply tell me what time it is?
- Ora - Hour

Heart Connection is the finale.

Learning and utilizing these easy Papiamento phrases will improve your Curaçao vacation experience by helping you to join in meaningful conversations and express your admiration for the local culture. When strangers attempt to converse in their language, locals are typically pleased. While English is commonly spoken, even a few Papiamento phrases may help you form bridges of understanding and create lasting memories of your visit to this wonderful island.

When it comes to visiting Curaçao, time is of the utmost importance. Throughout the year, the weather and dynamic activities on the island alter your experience, allowing a variety of chances for leisure, exploration, and cultural immersion.

Finding the Weather's Sweet Spot
Curaçao has a tropical environment with moderate temperatures throughout the year. The island has two different seasons:

The dry season lasts from January to September and is characterized by bright skies, low humidity, and negligible rain. It is considered the peak tourist season, with people traveling to Curaçao to enjoy the wonderful weather and clean waters, making it perfect for water-based activities such as snorkeling, diving, and swimming.

Rainy Season (October to December): Don't be scared off by the phrase "rainy season." Rainfall during this period is frequently brief and irregular, falling mostly at night or early in the morning. The island's natural surroundings blossom during this season, and the fewer people make it an intriguing choice for those wanting a more serene getaway.

Cultural immersion via events and festivals.

Curaçao's hectic schedule of events and festivals offers an added depth of excitement and cultural immersion to your visit:

Carnival (January-February): This vivid event lasts several weeks and culminates in magnificent parades, music, dancing, and bright costumes. Carnival creates a spectacular environment that embraces Curaçao's lively spirit.

Curaçao International Dive Event (September): This is a must-see event for diving aficionados. It provides a comprehensive diving experience by blending underwater exploration with educational programs, lectures, and conservation initiatives.

Curaçao North Sea Jazz Festival (August): Music connoisseurs travel to this world-known event, where famous performers play in a range of genres ranging from jazz to Latin and pop.

Dia di Bandera (July 2): This event celebrating Curaçao's flag day includes local customs, parades, and cultural activities that give insight into the island's rich past.

Se (December 26): This traditional dance and music festival, anchored in Curaçao's history and African heritage, gives a unique peek into native ceremonies and rhythms.

When it comes to tailoring your experience, time is essential.

Your interests and choices will define the perfect time to visit Curaçao:

High Season (January to August): The dry season is great for beachgoers, water enthusiasts, and those wanting a dynamic environment. Make lodging and activity arrangements in advance, because this time of year tends to bring more tourists.

Shoulder Season (September to November): This transitional season provides a beautiful blend of good weather, fewer tourists, and the chance to participate in local festivals and cultural activities.

Low Season (December): Visiting Curaçao during the rainy season allows you to see the island's natural beauty in a quieter atmosphere. While some establishments may have shortened their hours, you may still enjoy the island's beauty and partake in water sports throughout the rainy season.

Curaçao's varied environment and dynamic activities give a plethora of choices for all sorts of tourists. Whether you're searching for sun-soaked days, cultural activities, or tranquil escapes, each season has its allure. By tailoring your vacation to your interests and desired experiences, you can construct a memorable trip that displays the finest that this gorgeous Caribbean island has to offer.

Here are three example itineraries for various interests that highlight the range of experiences available in Curaçao:

Example 1 of an Itinerary: Beach Bliss and Water Adventures.

Day 1 starts with an arrival and a sunset joy.

Check into your beachside resort when you arrive in Curaçao.
Spend the day lounging on Mambo Beach's lovely beaches.
Enjoy a lovely sunset sail along the coast while enjoying beverages and admiring the amazing scenery.

On Day 2, there will be snorkeling and undersea beauty.

Spend the morning snorkeling in the gorgeous seas of Playa Lagun.
In the afternoon, visit the Curaçao Sea Aquarium for a close-up look at aquatic life.
In the evening, enjoy local cuisine at a beachside seafood restaurant.

Day 3: Scuba Diving Adventure

• Go on a diving adventure at the Tugboat Dive Site to observe the underwater wreck and vivid marine life.
• Spend the day lazing on Grote Knip Beach, noted for its magnificent blue waters.
• In the evening, meander about Willemstad's historic core, taking in the vivid buildings and waterfront vistas.

Day 4: Go island and beach hopping.
• Rent a jeep for an exciting off-road trip at Shete Boka National Park.
• Scuba dive with sea turtles in secret coves like Playa Piskado.
• A meal at Playa Porto Mari, where flamingos regularly assemble.

Departure and Scenic Cycling on Day 5
• Go on a guided bicycle tour of the picturesque hamlet of Scharloo.
• Try fresh tropical fruits at local markets.
• Take home lovely recollections of sun-kissed days and amazing water activities from Curaçao.

Cultural Immersion and Local Encounters is Itinerary.

Arrival and orientation on Day 1
• Upon arrival in Curaçao, check into your boutique hotel in Willemstad.
• Photograph the famous waterfront structures as you walk along Handelskade.
• Dine on true Krioyo food at a neighboring cafe.

The second day is dedicated to cultural exploration.
• Spend the morning visiting the Kura Hulanda Museum learning about the island's history and culture.
• In the afternoon, enjoy a visit to Landhuis Chobolobo and learn about the island's famed Blue Curaçao liquor.
• In the evening, wander around the Pietermaai District, which is noted for its lively street art and live music establishments.

Day 3: Meetings with Locals and Culinary Delights.
• Go on a guided village tour in Bandabou to meet artists and learn about local crafts.
• Participate in a culinary workshop where you will prepare traditional Papiamento treats.
• In the evening, visit Plasa Bieu, a local market providing a variety of traditional delicacies.

Day 4: Explore lovely towns.
• Visit Barber's village and meet with the residents to learn about their way of life.
• Visit Santa Martha for quiet beach views and a taste of traditional fishing techniques.
• An evening cultural dance performance at a local community facility.

Day 5: Farewell and Fond Memories
• Reminisce about your cultural experience over breakfast.
• Shop for souvenirs and handcrafted products at a local market.

• Leave Curaçao knowing more about its culture, customs, and people.

Itinerary 3 is an example of an active excursion and exploration of nature.

Day 1: Arrival and island orientation.
• Land in Curaçao and check into your natural eco-lodge.
• In the afternoon, take a guided walk in Christoffel National Park.
• Evening leisure with a view of the starlit heavens.

On Day 2, there will be mountain biking and waterfalls.
• Start the day with an exciting mountain bike ride in the hills near Soto.
• Go for a walk to Boka Tabla to observe the strength of the breaking waves against the rocks.
• An evening campfire and storytelling session at your eco-lodge.

Day 3 involves diving and marine exploration.
You may explore the underwater environment at the Mushroom Forest Dive Site.
Snorkel in Shete Boka National Park's natural waters, which are surrounded by rocky beauty.
To relax and connect with nature, try yoga on the beach at sunset.

Wildlife Encounters and Cave Exploration on Day 4.
Discover the geological and historical importance of the Hato Caves.

Kayak through the Spanish Water Lagoon, where mangroves and coastal birds may be spotted.
Evening nature stroll to watch sea turtles laying eggs on beaches.

Day 5: Farewell and Reflection
Spend the morning kayaking along the beach, soaking in the scenery.
• Reminisce about your active excursion over a goodbye picnic.
• Leave Curaçao feeling accomplished and with a profound respect for its natural treasures.

Finally, you can tailor your Curaçao experience.
Curaçao provides something for everyone, whether you're seeking beach pleasure, cultural immersion, or active adventure. These example itineraries are only a taste of the alternatives available, enabling you to construct a bespoke journey that reflects the charm of this great Caribbean island.

Travel Essentials and Packing List

Packing for your Curaçao vacation involves careful planning to ensure that you have everything you need for a comfortable and pleasurable trip. From beach necessities to practical goods, here's a detailed packing list to help you make the most of your time on this quaint Caribbean island.

Clothing:

• Summer attire that is lightweight and breathable (shorts, t-shirts, dresses, and skirts)
• Swimsuits and cover-ups for the beach
• Lightweight long-sleeve sun-protective shirts and trousers
• A hat or cap for sun protection
• Wear comfortable walking shoes or sandals for exploring.
• SPF lip balm and reef-safe sunscreen
• Sunglasses with UV protection

Outdoor Supplies:
• Snorkeling gear (if you have it)
• Water shoes for accessing rough beaches and indulging in aquatic activities
• A daypack or beach bag to keep necessities.
• Quick-drying beach towel
• Bug repellant for outdoor activities
• A reusable water jug for keeping hydrated.

Electronics:
• Smartphone cover for protection
• A waterproof smartphone case or backpack
• Chargers and power banks for your electronic devices
• Universal adapter (for charging reasons)

Health and First Aid:
• Prescription drugs and a copy of the prescriptions
• A first-aid kit (bandages, antiseptic wipes, pain medicines, and so on).
• Motion sickness cures (if necessary)

• Travel insurance details and emergency contact numbers

Money and paperwork:
• Passport photocopies
• Travel itinerary and lodging information on paper
• Credit/debit cards, as well as some cash (for modest local currency transactions).
• Travel wallet or bag for document organizing

Toiletries:
• Travel-sized toiletries (shampoo, conditioner, body wash, toothpaste)
• Floss and toothbrushes
• A hairbrush or comb
• Menstrual products (if necessary)
• A hand sanitizer

Clothing Accessories:
• A lightweight rain jacket or poncho (for unexpected rain).
• A light sweater or jacket for cold nights
• Swimsuits for beach excursions
• Pants and socks
• Nightgowns

Reading and amusement:
• Books on relaxation, journals, or e-books
• A journal or notepad to chronicle your experiences
• A pen or pencil for taking notes and scribbling down recollections

Extras Available:
• Snorkeling mask and fins (if available)
• A portable snorkel vest (for increased safety).
• A tiny umbrella (for sun or rain protection).
• Portable Bluetooth speaker for sitting by the pool or on the beach
• Beach toys or games (such as frisbee or paddleball)

Safety and hygiene:
• Face masks and hand sanitizer.
• Tampons, feminine hygiene products, and other feminine hygiene goods
• Prescription drugs and any essential medical supplies

Conclusion: Tailoring Your Packing to Your Preferences.

While this exhaustive list has everything you need, keep in mind that your packing should represent your particular interests and travel style.

Consider the activities you intend to undertake as well as any unique demands you may have. Remember that Curaçao has a laid-back and relaxed air, so pack comfortable clothes and accessories that complement the island's warm and friendly mood. If you plan ahead of time and pack smartly, you'll be well prepared to make the most of your excellent holiday to Curaçao.

A Journey of Experiences and Connections.

Curaçao is more than simply a destination; it's an invitation to embark on an experience of making lasting memories that will remain with you long after you've left its beaches. Curaçao provides a canvas for you to create your own unique and memorable experiences, from its stunning surroundings and vibrant culture to its warm-hearted people.

Sun-Kissed Beach Days: Imagine yourself reclining on powdered beaches, the turquoise seas providing a calming backdrop. The sun warms your skin as you enjoy the beauty of beaches such as Playa Kenepa, Cas Abao, and Grote Knip. Every swim, every sunbathing session, and every beach picnic full of laughter creates a vision of serenity and love.

Willemstad's Colorful Adventures: strolling around Willemstad is like strolling into a magnificent picture. With its pastel-colored buildings along the beach, the UNESCO-listed medieval city center dazzles. Capture the moment as you cross the historic Queen Emma Bridge and enter the magnificent Punda and Otrobanda lanes. The mix of Dutch colonial buildings with Caribbean flare offers a scene for numerous pictures and cultural connections.

Cultural Encounters and Genuine Connections: Interacting with the people of Curaçao is an extraordinary experience. Chatting with folks at Plasa Bieu, visiting art galleries, or taking a traditional dance lesson enables you to immerse yourself in the essence of the island and connect on a fundamental level. Sharing tales, laughing, and learning about local traditions improves and authenticates your experiences.

Dive into Underwater Wonders: Curaçao's underwater environment is a treasure mine of memories just waiting to be explored. Each diving and snorkeling trip offers a vast assortment of marine life, brilliant corals, and secret tunnels. Swimming with playful sea turtles or exploring the magnificent coral formations at Mushroom Forest will leave you in awe of the ocean's majesty.

culinary Delights & Flavorful Discoveries: Every meal in Curaçao is a gourmet adventure that exposes your taste buds to a range of tastes. Savoring Krioyo cuisine, fresh seafood, and tropical fruits creates memories entwined with the island's culinary tradition. Dining by the sea, sampling new dishes, and drinking drinks as the sun sets offers a vivid image of gastronomic delight.

Embracing Nature's Majesty: Exploring Curaçao's natural beauties, from the trails of Christoffel National Park to the steep slopes of Shete Boka, brings moments of amazement and connection to the land. Seeing the beautiful breaking waves, studying the island's peculiar birds, and finding secret beaches produce memories that help us appreciate the beauty of our surroundings.

Spectacular Sunsets & Starlit Nights: As the sun sets below the horizon, painting the sky orange and pink, you'll be mesmerized by the beauty of Curaçao's sunsets. These moments of calm and beauty, whether on a peaceful beach or atop a hill, are inscribed in your heart. As night falls, the stars fill the sky, offering a stunning background for evening walks and astronomy.

Curaçao is more than simply a holiday site; it's a tapestry of moments woven together to create a rich and vivid experience. Each touch, sight, taste, and experience becomes a brush stroke on this canvas of memories. Whether you're exploring its natural wonders, engaging with its culture, or simply basking in its beauty, the moments you create in Curaçao will become a cherished collection of memories that shape who you are and remind you of the extraordinary journey you undertook in this captivating Caribbean haven.

Bonus: Photography Tips On taking amazing photographs.

1. Leverage Golden Hour:
Capture the warm, soft light around dawn or sunset for lovely photos. The golden hour emphasizes the bright hues of Curaçao's surroundings.

2. Experiment with Perspectives:
Vary your angles and views. Capture photographs from varied heights, angles, and distances to add depth and intrigue to your photos.

3. Embrace Vibrant Colors:
Curaçao is recognized for its bright hues. Use the rich colors of the buildings, the water, and the landscapes to create visually spectacular compositions.

4. Utilize Rule of Thirds:
Divide your frame into thirds and position crucial items along these lines. This basic approach typically results in well-balanced and visually pleasing photographs.

5. Include Local Culture:
Capture the spirit of Curaçao by including local people, traditions, and events in your images. This adds dimension and gives a more full account of your journey.

6. Showcase Architecture:
Highlight the distinctive architectural appeal of Curaçao's buildings, notably those in Willemstad. Pay attention to details like the pastel hues and colonial influences.

7. Capture Underwater Beauty:
Invest in a nice underwater housing for your camera or use a waterproof smartphone to photograph the

beautiful marine life and coral reefs while snorkeling or diving.

8. Play with Reflections:
Take advantage of reflecting surfaces, such as the calm waters of Curaçao's bays, for compelling photos that include a wonderful play of light.

9. Master Low Light Photography:
Learn how to improve your camera or smartphone for low-light circumstances. This is particularly handy for capturing the exciting mood during Curaçao's nighttime festivities.

10. Focus on Details:
Zoom in on the minute things that make Curaçao special. Whether it's the textures of old buildings or the elaborate patterns of local crafts, details create a captivating tale.

11. Experiment with Silhouettes:
During sunset, try capturing silhouettes against the vivid sky. This method adds drama and intrigue to your photos.

12. Shoot in Burst Mode:
Capture fast-paced events, such as Carnival parades, by employing burst mode. This guarantees you grab the right moment among the frantic action.

13. Use Leading Lines:

Incorporate natural lines in the landscape or building to direct the viewer's gaze through the shot. This generates a feeling of depth and attracts attention to focus spots.

14. Be Mindful of Composition:
Compose your photos intelligently. Remove needless clutter, and ensure your topic is the focus point. Follow the law of simplicity.

15. Edit Thoughtfully:
Enhance your images using post-processing, but remember that subtlety is crucial. Adjust brightness, contrast, and color to edit your photographs without compromising the realism of the situation.

By combining these photography suggestions with the gorgeous scenery and rich culture of Curaçao, you'll be sure to take unforgettable photos throughout your vacation.

Printed in Great Britain
by Amazon

40292293R00066